RODALE ORGANIC

herbs

**From the Editors of
Rodale Organic Gardening
Magazine and Books**

RODALE

WE **INSPIRE** AND **ENABLE** PEOPLE TO IMPROVE
THEIR LIVES AND THE WORLD AROUND THEM

We're always happy to hear from you. For questions or comments concerning the editorial content of this book, please write to:

Rodale Book Readers' Service
33 East Minor Street
Emmaus, PA 18098

Look for other Rodale books wherever books are sold. Or call us at (800) 848-4735.

For more information about Rodale Organic Gardening magazine and books, visit us at:

www.organicgardening.com

Editor: Christine Bucks
Interior Book Designer: Nancy Smola Biltcliff
Interior Illustrator: Tony Davis
Cover Designer: Patricia Field
Cover Photographer: Steven Foster Group/ Martin Wall
Photography Editor: Lyn Horst
Photography Assistant: Jackie L. Ney
Layout Designer: Dale Mack
Researcher: Diana Erney
Copy Editor: Erana Bumbardatore
Manufacturing Coordinator: Patrick T. Smith
Indexer: Nan N. Badgett
Editorial Assistance: Kerrie A. Cadden

RODALE ORGANIC GARDENING BOOKS
Executive Editor: Kathleen DeVanna Fish
Managing Editor: Fern Marshall Bradley
Executive Creative Director: Christin Gangi
Art Director: Patricia Field
Production Manager: Robert V. Anderson Jr.
Studio Manager: Leslie M. Keefe
Copy Manager: Nancy N. Bailey
Manufacturing Manager: Eileen F. Bauder

Library of Congress
  Cataloging-in-Publication Data
    Rodale organic gardening basics. Volume 5, Herbs / from the editors of Rodale organic gardening magazine and books.
        p. cm.
    Includes bibliographical references and index.
    ISBN 0-87596-854-6 (pbk. : alk. paper)
    1. Herb gardening. 2. Herbs. 3. Organic gardening. I. Title: Herbs. II. Rodale Books. III. Organic gardening (Emmaus, Pa. : 1988) IV. Rodale organic gardening basics ; v. 5.
SB351.H5 R577 2001
635'.7—dc21   00-009597

Distributed in the book trade by St. Martin's Press

2 4 6 8 10 9 7 5 3 1   paperback

contents

Backyard Magic

Herbs may seem magical and mysterious, considering their legendary healing powers, strong flavors, and intoxicating fragrances. But they are really a gardener's best friend, providing easy-to-grow beauty that looks great all summer long.

In fact, many herbs are just as beautiful as the other annuals and perennials that grace your garden beds, but the beauty of herbs is more than skin deep. Lots of them taste amazing, especially when you pick them right outside your kitchen door while dinner is cooking (think basil, parsley, and cilantro). And many of them make delicious teas. Nothing is more refreshing than fresh-picked mint iced tea in the summer . . . just pick some mint, pour boiling water over it, put it in the refrigerator to cool, strain the tea, and then enjoy. As an added bonus, mint tea will soothe a troubled tummy.

And the fragrance of herbs! Lavender, creeping thyme, and chamomile all fill the air with the romantic scents of summer.

I plant herbs throughout my landscape for their beauty, taste, and fragrance, and I couldn't imagine a garden without them.

Buying fresh herbs in the supermarket can be expensive—but growing your own is a real bargain. And once you've had fresh-picked herbs, you'll be amazed at how much better they taste and smell. This book will show you all you need to know to make your garden an herbal delight . . . just like magic.

Happy organic gardening!

Maria Rodale

Maria Rodale

> **Herbs are a gardener's best friend, providing easy-to-grow beauty that looks great all summer long.**

Herbs can add color, texture, and fragrance to your landscape—as well as provide food and shelter for good bugs.

chapter one

Go Organic: Growing Herbs Simplified

Herbs are incredibly versatile plants. You can incorporate them into your landscape, kitchen garden, or flowerbeds, or you can grow them in pots on your patio or indoors on a sunny windowsill. They make great flavorings, fragrances, medicines, teas, and crafts. And most herbs demand little attention, making them easy plants to grow organically.

EASY ORGANIC HERBS

There's no reason not to grow herbs organically—they don't need pesticides or herbicides to grow and produce well. You'll have little trouble with disease or insect damage if you grow your plants out in the sun and wind. And by gardening organically, you'll create a natural balance between the soil, plants, and insects, and that balance will result in healthier plants. That means you'll have a lot more time to enjoy the fruits of your labors, whether it's by drinking a steaming cup of chamomile tea or by making your own herbal potpourri.

Most herbs demand little attention, making them easy plants to grow organically.

3 Things You Can STOP Doing Now

The first step in switching to gardening organically is just to stop doing some chores that aren't necessary or are actually harmful. So whether you've grown herbs before or are trying it for the first time, check out this list of things you can *stop* doing when you grow herbs the organic way.

1. STOP Using Chemicals!

All good gardens start with healthy soil, and your soil will start getting healthier as soon as you stop using pesticides, herbicides, and synthetic fertilizers. If you put chemicals on your garden, they leach into the soil, which can harm the microorganisms and beneficial insects (the good guys) that live there. You want to keep those good bugs alive so there will be lots of them around to pollinate plants and eat pest insects. Also, when you put chemicals on culinary herbs, it means you'll be ingesting those chemicals, which you don't want to do.

2. STOP **Planting without Planning!**

Planning to grow herbs is a two-step process. The first part involves thinking about what you want to use your herbs for and then planting the right herbs for those uses. For example, if you're interested in growing culinary herbs, basil and dill would be good choices, rather than an herb like catnip.

Before you plant any herbs, think about what you want to use them for. Basil, for example, is an excellent culinary herb.

BRINGING IN THE BENEFICIALS

BESIDES THE BEAUTY they add to the garden, herbs offer another important benefit—they provide food and shelter for beneficial insects. Beneficial insects are the bugs that eat bad bugs (or the eggs or larvae of bad bugs). And having beneficial insects hanging out in your garden is an important part of organic pest control.

What makes herbs so attractive to beneficials? Well, some herbs—such as coriander, dill, fennel, and parsley—have flat flower heads that resemble miniature umbrellas. This special type of flower head is called an umbel, and it's actually composed of many clusters of very tiny flowers. Parasitic wasps and other beneficial insects can reach the nectar in these individual flowers easily and then go on to parasitize troublesome caterpillars, such as tomato hornworms. Other beneficial insects such as syrphid flies and green lacewings also nourish themselves on these flowers before laying their eggs, which will then hatch into voracious, aphid-eating larvae. And lady beetles rely on the flowers of dill and yarrow to supplement their diet when their favorite food—aphids—is in short supply.

Beneficial insects also feed on the flowers of bergamot, lavender, mints, and thyme. To keep these helpful guests on pest patrol in your garden, try to have at least one of their favorite flowers in bloom throughout the growing season.

The second part of planning involves choosing the right site. Matching the right herb to the right garden conditions goes a long way toward growing healthy, vigorous plants. That means placing heat lovers, like basil, in full sun, and moisture lovers, like mint, in damp spots.

3. STOP Killing Every Caterpillar You Find!

Even though pest insects don't usually bother herb plants, that doesn't mean you won't have some bad bugs hanging around your garden. But you'll have good guys hanging out, too—bugs who may actually help your garden. So the next time you see a caterpillar in your garden bed, take some time to find out what it is before you decide whether it warrants being squashed.

Having the right tools on hand will help you produce a gorgeous garden of herbs.

chapter two

Tools & Supplies

One of the great things about herbs is that they're very low-maintenance plants. They're not overly fussy about growing conditions, and they have little trouble with diseases and insect pests. So that means you don't need a wide array of tools and supplies to care for them. A few essentials for planting, weeding, and harvesting are all it takes to help you grow a bountiful garden of herbs.

QUALITY AND CARE

Although you don't need a lot of tools to care for herbs, the ones you do use should be of good quality. They'll last longer and help you do a better job than less-expensive or poorer-quality tools will.

Before you buy, check out the handles of the tools you want. Wood handles are strong and durable, and they feel good in your hands. Over time, they will wear slightly to become smoother where you hold them. Fiberglass handles are lighter and stronger than wood. Also, for any tool that you'll use standing up, such as a hoe or a shovel, make sure that the handle is at least shoulder height.

Be sure to look at the working end of digging and cultivating tools, too. They should be made of one solid piece of rustproof or rust-resistant metal.

Of course, there's no point in buying good-quality tools if you're not going to take care of them, so be sure to clean your tools after each use. Use a plastic or wooden spatula to knock or scrape soil off metal blades. (Don't use the metal blade of one tool to clean another—you might end up damaging both.) Remove any remaining soil with a wire brush or by spraying the tool with a hose. When the tool is completely clean and dry, wipe the metal with an oily cloth to prevent rust.

5 Essential Herb Gardening Tools

- **Trowel**
- **Hoe**
- **Shovel or spade**
- **Cultivator**
- **Pruning shears**

Trowel

HAND TOOLS

You don't need special tools to grow herbs—the same tools you use for vegetables and flowers will work just fine.

Trowel

A good trowel is an indispensable garden tool. You'll need one for transplanting young herbs and preparing small areas before seeding. Trowels also work well for adding small amounts of soil amendments into planting holes. Choose a sturdy trowel that won't bend when you exert pressure on it and that has a handle that feels comfortable in your hand. Trowels have a way of losing themselves in the garden, but if you paint the handle a bright color, you'll be able to find your trowel again easily if you happen to walk off and leave it behind.

Shovels and Spades

Most herb gardens start at the end of a shovel or spade. Which one should you use to start your garden? You probably already own a shovel, and it's the tool of choice if you'll be breaking hard ground. Shovels have long handles that end in a blade that is somewhat concave with a rounded, yet slightly pointed end. They're great for digging dirt out of planting holes and for scooping up compost, sand, and other soil amendments.

Spades have flat, rectangular blades and shorter handles with D-shaped grips. Leverage and a sharp blade make a spade a great choice for digging garden

Shovel

Spade

beds. You simply push the blade into the soil, put your foot on one side of the blade, then lean back on the handle to lift the soil. The sharp edge of a spade's blade also makes quick work of edging an established bed or chopping off errant weeds you happen by on your way back to the toolshed.

Hoes

Once your herb bed is established, you'll need a good hoe to keep it tidy and weed-free. The classic American hoe has a square blade with round shoulders. You can use it in your herb garden, but it's really better suited for big jobs in the vegetable garden. Hoes with smaller blades and sharp edges—such as the collinear hoe, Winged Weeder, and Warren hoe—navigate around plants more easily, slicing through tough weed roots as they go.

Hand-Pruning Shears

Once you own a good set of pruners, you'll wonder how you ever got along without them. You'll need a pair for harvesting herbs throughout the season (although you can get by with an ordinary pair of kitchen scissors for harvesting herbs that don't have very thick stems). Pruners also come in handy in fall, when you'll be cutting back perennial herbs to prepare them for winter. Most serious gardeners prefer bypass pruners, which have blades that work like scissors, rather than anvil-type pruners, which have a sharp blade that closes against a metal plate. Whichever type you choose, make sure the handles feel good in your hand. The latch that holds the blades together when they're not in use should unlock easily, and the blades should open and close smoothly when you squeeze the handles.

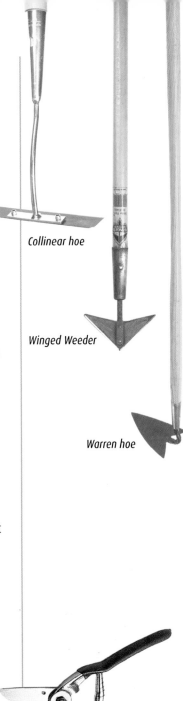

Collinear hoe

Winged Weeder

Warren hoe

Bypass pruners

Hand Cultivator

A handheld cultivator looks kind of like a claw. It has three curved tines on the end that work well for breaking up compacted soil and clearing away weeds in established herb and perennial beds. Cultivators are also helpful when you're working small amounts of compost or other soil amendments into the soil around plants.

Hand cultivator

MAINTENANCE AND HARVESTING EQUIPMENT

Once your herbs are in the ground, you'll need a few more items to help you maintain your garden and reap the fruits of your labors.

Plastic Buckets or Nursery Pots

Given half a chance, boisterous herbs like mints will run amok in the garden. To keep these overexuberant growers in line, create a barrier around plantings using old buckets or nursery pots. Simply cut the bottoms out of the pots, then work the pots into the soil around the plantings, leaving just an inch or two above the soil line so that rampant roots can't work

Plastic nursery pots create an excellent— and inexpensive— barrier for exuberant herbs like mint.

their way over the wall. For larger plantings, you may need more than one pot or bucket—slit them down one side and you'll be able to open them up and arrange them end to end around a planting.

Gathering Baskets

Of course, as you harvest your herbs, you could just place them in any old container you have laying around the kitchen. But since you've gone to all the trouble of growing them yourself, why not harvest them in style with a nice gathering basket? Choose a basket with low sides and a flat bottom so that you can layer the herbs inside without crushing them. If you really want to harvest English country garden–style, buy yourself a trug—a flat, rectangular harvesting basket with wooden slats on the bottom and a sturdy wooden handle.

When harvesting herbs, use a basket with low sides and a flat bottom, like this one. That way, you can layer the herbs without crushing them.

CONTAINERS

Just because you don't have a lot of space doesn't mean you can't grow herbs. All you need is the right container to grow your plants in, and you can have a lovely windowsill or patio herb garden. You'll also need the right container if you plan on bringing garden-grown herbs indoors for the winter.

When choosing your pots, keep in mind that you'll want containers that will provide adequate space and drainage for their future inhabitants, in addition to looking attractive.

To help you decide which pot to buy, ask yourself these two questions:

Do you want to use your pot indoors or out? Generally speaking, if you're planning on growing herbs outdoors, you'll need a container that can hold 2 to 4 gallons of growing medium. Herbs don't grow as

LOW-BUDGET LABELS

PLANT LABELS are pretty much a necessity if you're planting lots of different types of herbs and you want to remember what you've planted where. But you don't have to spend a lot of extra money on labels; you can make your own with an indelible marker and some stuff you probably already have around your house. Here are some ideas:

- Cut old miniblind slats into 6-inch pieces and write herb names on them.

- Save the plastic labels from store-bought plants. Clean off the words with a scrubbing pad, and write a new plant label.

- Save those free paint stirrers that you get at the hardware store and write herb names on them.

- Wash off Popsicle sticks (after you've eaten the ice cream, of course), and turn them into plant labels.

No matter what type of pot you choose for your herbs, make sure it has a drainage hole in the bottom.

vigorously indoors, so you can use much smaller pots if you're planning on having a windowsill herb garden.

What is your preferred container made out of?
Containers made of clay or terra-cotta look pretty, and they're weighty enough to keep your patio herbs from tumbling over during stormy weather. But clay pots are porous and dry out quickly on hot summer days, so you'll need to water herbs in these pots more often. Plastic pots hold moisture much longer. They're also lighter and easier to move around, so they're a good choice if you'll be moving your pots in and out of doors with the changing seasons.

Whatever pot you choose, make sure it has a drainage hole—plant roots will suffocate and rot if they sit in water too long. You can use pots without holes and unusual items like buckets (or even old boots) for planters if you drill a ½-inch hole in the bottom before filling them. Another way to use these types of containers is to put your plant into a slightly smaller pot that already has drainage holes, and then place that smaller pot inside the planter. Elevate the smaller pot by placing a few blocks of wood in the base of the planter. If the pot is outdoors, you may need to remove the plant and dump the water out of the planter during rainy spells.

COMPOST AND MULCH

Compost and mulch are as important to making herbs happy as they are to making vegetables happy. That's because these ingredients supply nutrients to the soil, help keep the soil moist, and suppress weeds.

Compost

Next to sunlight and water, quality compost is one of the most important things that you can give your garden. Compost is an excellent fertilizer, providing a well-balanced diet of nutrients to your plants.

Work compost into the top 4 to 6 inches of soil when establishing new beds, and you'll improve your soil structure, which will in turn improve soil drainage. Homemade compost is usually the best quality. But, if you're not able to make your own, pay a visit to your local yard-waste recycling center and you can probably haul away as much as your vehicle can carry for free (or at worst, a nominal loading fee). Be discriminating when buying bagged composts because the quality can vary widely. Mature compost should be dark brown, crumbly, and smell like the good Earth. Avoid composts that are clumpy or gooey or that have suspicious odors.

A 1-inch layer of compost on top of the soil is a great mulch, helping to retain soil moisture and suppress weeds.

Mulch

Once your garden bed is prepared and your herbs are in the ground, it's a good idea to tuck them in with a layer of mulch. You'll spend less time weeding, since weeds have a tough time sprouting and growing through a thick layer of mulch. A protective mulch will also help the soil retain precious moisture and keep plant roots cooler during summer hot spells. Shredded bark and compost are attractive choices, and they also provide food to your soil and plants.

A garden right outside your back door is the perfect spot for growing culinary herbs.

chapter three

Planning Your Herb Garden

The hardest part of herb gardening can be deciding what kind of herbs you want to grow—and then deciding where you're going to grow them. Do you want herbs for crafts or for cooking? Do you have sunny or shady sites? And what other plants grow well with herbs? Once you answer these questions, you'll be on your way to getting your herb garden off to a good start.

HERBS FOR COOKING

If you're just starting with herbs, or if you don't have a lot of garden space, you'll probably want to stick with basic culinary herbs. Homegrown herbs straight from the garden offer the freshest flavors—something you just can't get from store-bought herbs. It's also easy to dry herbs at home; their savory flavors will linger to add a taste of summer to midwinter meals.

A broad range of herbs is available to add flavor to everything from salad dressings to desserts. Here's a list of some popular herbs and how you can use them to liven up meals.

- Basil (with meats or vegetables, in sauces)
- Chervil (in soups or stews, or with fish or vegetables)
- Chives (in soups, salads, and sandwiches)
- Dill (with fish or vegetables; in salads or sauces; seeds used for pickling)
- French tarragon (in salads or sauces; with meats, fish, or vegetables)

Homegrown herbs straight from the garden offer fresh flavors you just can't get from store-bought herbs.

- Garlic (with most anything, except desserts)
- Lovage (use like celery in soups, stews, salads, or sauces)
- Oregano (in sauces or with cheeses, eggs, meats, or vegetables)
- Parsley (with most anything, except desserts)
- Rosemary (with meats or vegetables; in soups or sauces)
- Sage (with eggs, poultry, or vegetables)
- Sweet marjoram (use like oregano)
- Thyme (with meats or vegetables)

Hints for Herbal Cooking

Fresh and dried homegrown herbs are interchangeable in most recipes. Dried herbs are more powerful, ounce for ounce, than fresh ones, so when substituting fresh herbs for dried, use two or three times more. To release the flavor of dried herbs, crush the foliage between your hands before adding it to recipes.

Most herbs don't require cooking; add them just before taking the dish off the stove. Or, for the freshest flavor, simply add a pinch of herbs to each plate at serving time. If you're using a specific herb for the first time, use restraint when adding it to a dish. If you overdo it, you might overwhelm the original flavor of the meat or vegetable that you meant to enhance.

Fresh basil is great for livening up vegetables and meats.

If you do find that you've been a little heavy-handed with the seasoning, try these tips.

- Strain as much of the herbs and spices as possible out of the dish.
- Add a peeled, whole, raw potato to the pot just before serving.
- If possible, add more of the nonherb ingredients, or make a second, unseasoned batch of the recipe and combine it with the overseasoned one.
- Serve the dish chilled to blunt the taste of the over-seasoning.

HERBS FOR CRAFTS

Making craft projects with herbs is a creative and delightful way to bring your garden indoors. You can work with fresh and dried herbs rich with color, texture, and fragrance to make wreaths, potpourris, and fragrant oils. The number of ways you can use herbs in crafts is really only limited by your imagination.

Many common herbs are great for craft projects. Here are a few ideas.

- Create a culinary wreath using chives, creeping sage, marjoram, oregano, or thyme.
- Braid fresh garlic heads together with bunches of herbs, then hang them to dry in the kitchen. Later, use scissors to cut away the bulbs or dried herbs as they're needed for cooking.

You can create a unique fragrant wreath using a variety of herbs from your garden.

SELECTING HERBS

ONCE YOU KNOW what you want your herbs for, you can choose specific kinds. Look for species that are adapted to the conditions your garden has to offer (most herbs do well in average, well-drained soil with full sun). Experiment with different varieties of herbs to find out which ones grow best in your climate. Some herbs even have varieties that lend themselves best to specific uses. For example, you can choose dill varieties that produce lots of foliage for tossing with salads or dill varieties that produce lots of seeds to add to tasty pickle recipes.

If you're new to herb growing, you'll probably find all the choices you need at your local garden center. Read the seed packets or the plant labels to find out the traits of each herb you're considering. As you gain experience and want to grow more varieties, start looking at specialty seed and plant catalogs. (See "Seeds, Plants & Supplies" on page 100 for a list of catalogs.)

- Create a personalized potpourri by mixing together your favorite dried herbs, flowers, and spices. Mint, rosemary, sage, and thyme are just a few of the herbs that hold their fragrances well when dried.
- Use herbs like oregano and yarrow in fresh or dried arrangements.
- Instead of bows, add small bunches of dried and leafy herbs like thyme or sage to wrapped gifts.

HERBS FOR FRAGRANCE

Flowers release their scents into the air so freely that you need only walk past roses, lilacs, or any other highly fragrant blooms to enjoy their aromas. Herbs, on the other hand, don't usually release their

Rub the leaves of scented geraniums to release their fragrance.

scents unless you rub a leaf, walk on the plant, or brush against the herb's branches. But that doesn't mean you can't grow and enjoy herbs specifically for their fragrances—and there are certainly enough fragrant herbs to choose from.

The leaves of scented geraniums, for instance, smell wonderful when you rub them. They come in a wide variety of scents, including ginger, lemon, lemon-rose, mint, nutmeg, and rose. Scented geraniums, along with lavender (floral scent), lemon balm (citrusy scent), lemon verbena (citrusy scent), and sweet woodruff (woodsy/earthy scent), are among the best-known herbs for fragrance.

You can use fragrant herbs many different ways, such as by creating these household items.

<table>
<tr><td>

quick tip

For the ultimate fragrant, relaxing bath, place a handful of dried lemon balm—along with other soothing herbs, such as chamomile and catnip—in a small muslin bag or oversize tea ball, and drop them into your warm bath water.
</td></tr>
</table>

- Sachets
- Pomanders
- Herb pillows
- Essential oils
- Perfumes
- Scented candles
- Scented soaps

HERBS FOR TEA

Of all the things you can do with herbs, one of the most popular is making and drinking herbal tea. Historically, herbal teas were used as medicines, and many people still brew and drink them for their medicinal effects. But most people drink herbal teas because they find them soothing. You can brew a tasty pot from of any of the following herbs (use leaves only, unless otherwise noted):

- Angelica
- Bee balm
- Catnip (leaves and flowers)
- Chamomile (flowers)
- Lemon balm
- Lemon thyme
- Lemon verbena
- Mints
- Rosemary
- Sage
- Scented geraniums

You can use either fresh or dried herbs to make a relaxing cup of herbal tea.

Keep in mind that not all herbs are suitable for making tea. Do some research before you brew.

Brewing the Perfect Pot of Tea

Herbal teas are at their best when brewed lightly and delicately, and they can be made with either dried or fresh herbs. To make herbal tea, you'll need 1 teaspoon of dried herbs or 1 tablespoon of fresh herbs for each 6- to 8-ounce cup. Place the herbs in a china, pottery, or other nonmetal teapot (nonmetal pots help keep the tea pure in flavor and hot while it brews). Add boiling water and let the tea steep for 5 to 10 minutes (keep the pot covered to retain heat). Steeping time will vary, depending on what herbs you're using, so do taste checks at regular intervals until you're sure. Then strain the herbs out and serve the tea with honey, lemon, orange slices, or fresh herb sprigs.

Making Iced Tea

You can also make delicious iced tea using the same procedure as above, except use 3 tablespoons of fresh herbs or 2 tablespoons of dried herbs for each 6- to 8-ounce cup. (The extra amount of herbs will keep your tea from becoming diluted as the ice melts.)

For a change of pace, try freezing herb teas in ice cube trays and using the cubes to chill refreshing summer drinks, such as lemonade or punch—or to add sparkle to plain water. You can also freeze sprigs of herbs, like mint, in ice cubes for flavoring and decorating beverages.

quick tip

Who says you can't mix and match herbs in teas? Try any of the combinations below to find your favorite.

- Spearmint, elderberry, and lemon balm
- Lemon verbena and borage
- Savory, lemongrass, and scented geranium
- Chamomile and apple mint

HERBS FOR HEALING

Herbs are also traditional ingredients in many home remedies. While natural food stores and vitamin suppliers sell all sorts of ready-made herbal medicines, it's less expensive and more satisfying to make your own remedies with herbs picked right from your garden. You can combine the herbs to fit your own needs and tastes and make just the right amounts you need. And by growing herbs organically, you can guarantee their purity because you'll know they won't have been treated with any chemicals.

Just remember that many herbs have toxic properties, and some are absolutely poisonous. That's why it's extremely important to

- make sure each plant is correctly identified before you use it;

- use all plants judiciously;

- remember that medicines that are healthful when taken in small quantities can be very harmful when taken in larger doses;

- avoid mixing herbal remedies with prescription medications; and

- consult a doctor about a serious ailment instead of trying to treat it yourself.

7 Top Herbs

Here are seven herbs you can grow in your garden along with the conditions they cure.

Basil wastes warts. This aromatic herb contains many antiviral compounds. One widely practiced folk remedy for warts involves rubbing crushed basil leaves on the growths.

Calendula treats cuts and scrapes. It reduces inflammation and heals wounds. The flowers are used externally in infusions (teas brewed for anywhere from 15 minutes to several hours), ointments, and tinctures.

Chamomile battles gingivitis. Chamomile is effective as a gargle or mouthwash for treating gingivitis. That's because its flowers contain several anti-inflammatory and antiseptic compounds.

Fennel eases asthma. The Greeks treated asthma and other respiratory ailments with fennel tea. Fennel contains a helpful chemical that helps loosen bronchial secretions.

Garlic relieves insect bites and stings. It contains enzymes that break down chemical substances that the body releases in response to pain. Interestingly enough, garlic works both internally and externally. You can make a poultice and apply it directly to insect bites and stings, or you can get a measure of relief by eating garlic.

Garlic is more than just a culinary herb. You can also use it to relieve insect stings.

Lemon balm alleviates migraines. The recommended dose is a tea made with 1 to 2 teaspoons of dried herb per cup of boiling water, steeped until cool.

Parsley beats bad breath. Bright green parsley is a rich source of chlorophyll, which is a powerful breath freshener.

PLANNING YOUR HERB GARDEN

Once you've decided what herbs you want to grow, you need to figure out where you're going to put them. If you just want to grow a few herbs, you may decide to tuck them into a flowerbed or the vegetable garden. If you really want to get into growing and using herbs, you'll probably want to create a separate garden for them. Either way, here are a few points to keep in mind.

Match Plants to Place

For healthy, vigorous herbs, give your plants the best possible conditions. Although many herbs can adapt to poor, dry soil, that doesn't mean they thrive in it; fertile, well-prepared garden soil will encourage much better growth. And as we mentioned back in Chapter 1, be sure to match each herb to the right garden conditions.

Leave Room to Grow

Just like vegetables, herbs need room to spread without crowding their neighbors. For the right spacing, follow the guidelines on the seed packets or transplant labels. Crowding in lots of herbs won't give you a better harvest; instead, the plants won't grow as well, and you'll be left with lots of thinning and dividing work to keep plants healthy.

If you're growing perennial herbs that will spread—such as mint—plan some kind of containment system, or soon you'll have nothing but the spreaders. Or set aside a separate area of the garden where they can spread without endangering more delicate plants.

FUN FACT

HERE'S A SHORT LIST OF HERBS AND THEIR TRADITIONAL MEANINGS.

BASIL—LOVE, GOOD WISHES
CHAMOMILE—WISDOM, FORTITUDE
CHERVIL—SINCERITY
CHIVES—USEFULNESS
DILL—GOOD CHEER
FENNEL—GRIEF, POWER,
 AND ENDURANCE
SCENTED GERANIUM—HAPPINESS

You don't need to grow herbs in a special "herb" garden. You can always stick a few here and there among your flowers and vegetables.

Pick a Practical Site

While it's important to give your herbs the conditions they like, you'll also want to consider your needs. For example, you're most likely to use your herbs if they're close to the house. Also, plan your garden for easy care. You can do that by

- choosing a site near a water supply (for moisture-loving herbs like mint);

- allowing for paths so you can comfortably reach into all parts of the garden without stepping on the soil; and

- making at least one path wide enough so you can get into the center of a large garden with tools and a wheelbarrow.

COMPANION PLANTING

Companion planting is planting certain combinations of plants together to repel pests, attract beneficial insects, or make efficient use of garden beds. You can use herbs in companion plantings to repel or trap pests and to help other plants grow.

Herbs That Beat Pests

Try planting garlic with bush beans to repel aphids, and catnip with eggplant to repel flea beetles. A ring of chives under an apple tree is said to discourage apple scab. Other herbs used to repel pests include:

- Anise hyssop
- Borage
- Calendula
- Cilantro
- Dill

- Mint
- Rosemary
- Sage
- Scented geranium
- Tansy

You can also use herbs as traps to lure pests away from your crops. Dill and lovage can be used to lure hornworms from tomatoes, for example.

quick tip

Most herbs grow best in sun and average, well-drained soil, but not all gardens can offer these ideal conditions. Here are some herbs that can adapt to less-than-perfect sites.

Shade-tolerant herbs. Bay, bee balm, chamomile, chervil, comfrey, ginger, lemon balm, mint, and sweet woodruff

Herbs for moist spots. Angelica, borage, comfrey, ginger, horseradish, lovage, mint, and sweet cicely

Herbs for dry spots. Anise, catnip, tarragon, and thyme

Herbs That Help

Some herbs seem to enhance the growth of other plants. Try pairing borage with strawberries, chervil with radishes, sage with cabbage-family crops, and summer or winter savory with onions. Also try basil or thyme around tomatoes, and tarragon with any vegetable you're growing. (Watch out, though: Some herbs inhibit neighboring plants. Dill, for example, slows the growth of tomatoes, while garlic harms neighboring beans and peas.)

Basil not only tastes great when paired with tomatoes, but it also seems to enhance a tomato plant's growth.

How to Use Companions

You can mix and match herbs with most other plants, as long as you're meeting the growth requirements of each individual plant. Here are some guidelines to follow when choosing companions.

- Choose companion plants that have the same requirements for sunlight, water, season, and temperature.

- Plant perennial herbs with perennial crops. You can pair strawberries and Roman chamomile or lemon thyme in the same bed. Or let asparagus share space with tarragon. You can sow seeds of shallow-rooted annual herbs, such as cilantro or dill, around established perennial fruits and vegetables, but don't dig holes and set-in plants—you'll disturb the root system of the perennial.

- Avoid using invasive herbs, such as mint, as companion plants, because they'll quickly take over. Instead, grow invasive herbs in pots near the garden.

Starting with plants, as opposed to seeds, is a fast and easy way to have an instant herb garden.

chapter four

Planting & Caring for Herbs

Once you've decided what herbs you want to grow, it's time to get your hands into the soil. In this chapter, you'll learn what you need to do when starting with plants or seeds. You'll also discover how to control herbs that grow out of bounds and how you can keep herbs thriving indoors when Old Man Winter arrives.

STARTING WITH PLANTS

Buying plants is the way to go if you want to start with just a few of each herb. Buying plants is also a good choice for perennial herbs. For the best success, buy the following herbs as plants (unless otherwise indicated):

- Garlic (bulbs)
- Scented geranium
- Horseradish (roots)
- Lavender
- Lovage
- Mint
- Oregano
- Rosemary
- Sage
- Tarragon
- Thyme

Start with only one or two plants to see how well they do in your conditions and how well you like them. You can always buy more plants next year.

Sniffing Before You Buy

Knowledgeable herb gardeners sniff before they buy. That's because many specialty herbs—including oregano and French tarragon—don't come true from seed. Seedlings may have no fragrance whatsoever,

> **For your first herb garden, buy just one or two herb plants to see how well they do in your conditions.**

25

Always sniff an herb plant before you buy it to find out if it has the full-blown aroma you're looking for.

or they may only be a weak facsimile of the best culinary aromas. Don't buy plants hoping they'll develop fragrance and flavor as they grow because they won't. Even small plants should have the full-blown, pungent aromas the herbs are grown for. To test a plant's aroma, gently rub a leaf between your fingers and take a good whiff.

STARTING FROM SEED

Growing herbs from seed is less expensive, but it takes more time and care than buying plants. As a general rule, growing from seed is best for annuals and biennials. It's also a good choice when you want more than just a plant or two. You can either directly sow herb seeds in the ground or sow them in pots indoors.

Herbs for direct sowing. You can sow these herbs directly in the garden: basil, borage, German chamomile, chervil, cilantro, dill, fennel, mustard, and parsley.

Herbs for indoor sowing. For an extra-early crop, start basil, sweet marjoram, and parsley indoors. For a continuous supply of fresh herbs, sow a second crop outdoors when soil temperatures warm up.

Easy perennials from seed. Catnip, chives, feverfew, and lemon balm are easy to grow from seed sown indoors or out.

PLANTING HERBS

Plant annual herbs just as you would plant vegetables. Since perennial herbs will grow in your garden for several years or more, take extra care to get them off to a good start. Plant them in spring or fall, when temperatures are cool and the soil has lots of moisture in it. Overcast days are best for planting because plants will have time to recover from the shock of moving from their cozy homes in pots to their new home in the garden.

Here's a three-step approach to getting your herbs in the ground.

1. **Prepare for planting.** Give your herbs a good drink before you plant by soaking them, pots and all, in a shallow tub of water, weak compost tea, or liquid seaweed solution. When you're ready to plant, pinch away any dead stems, leaves, and spent blossoms, and pull and throw away weed seedlings growing in the pot. Then dig a hole that's deep enough so you can set the plant at the same depth it grew at in the pot.

2. **Remove plants from pots.** To remove a plant from its pot, hold one hand over the top of the pot with your fingers around the stem. Turn the pot upside down with the other hand, and tap the bottom. Then gently squeeze the plant out of the pot while keeping the ball of soil and roots intact. Loosen roots that are tightly intertwined, and cut away bent or broken ones.

3. **Settle plants in the soil.** Center the plant in the hole, making sure it is sitting at the same depth that it was in the pot. Plants planted too deeply can rot; those planted

When removing a plant from a pot, make sure one hand is securely holding the plant around its stems.

too shallowly can dry out. After setting the plant, replace the soil. Firm the soil around the stems, forming a shallow trench around the center stem to hold water and direct it to the plant's roots. Water gently and thoroughly. Apply an organic mulch such as cocoa bean hulls to keep plant leaves clean and to help retain soil moisture.

quick tip

Perennial herbs are ideal problem solvers in the landscape. Since many will grow well in hot, dry sites, use them as groundcovers on a hard-to-mow slope or as an edging along a fence or tough-to-trim spot. Herbs are also a good choice for filling in rocky sites. They'll serve as a permanent mulch, hold the soil, and outcompete weeds. Chamomile, lavender, oregano, and thyme are good choices for sites with dry soils. Try sweet woodruff in wet spots.

CONTROLLING INVASIVE HERBS

Some perennial herbs, such as horseradish and mint, grow so vigorously that they'll engulf their better-behaved neighbors. Here are some control tactics to use on them.

- **Impermeable mulch.** Mulch around invasive herbs with a 1-inch-thick layer of newspaper. Cover the newspaper with an attractive mulch like cocoa bean hulls or bark chips. Renew this mulch combination each season to prevent the spread of invasive herbs.

- **Herbal islands.** Plant invasive herbs in island beds, surrounded by lawn. Weekly mowing around the beds will keep the spreaders in check.

- **Sunken containers.** Plant invasive herbs in large containers sunk into the soil to keep roots from spreading through the entire bed (see "Containing Creepers," below).

Containing Creepers

If you plant an invasive herb in a bucket, the roots can't get through the bucket walls, and the bucket rim stops creeping stems that spread along the soil surface. (Trim away stems that sneak over the top.) Here's how to do it.

1. Use a hammer and nail to punch several drainage holes in the bottom of a large bucket. Five-gallon plastic buckets are ideal.

2. Dig a hole in the soil that fits the bucket. The hole should be deep enough so that when you put the bucket in the soil, the rim sticks up 3 to 4 inches above the soil surface.

3. Put the bucket in the hole and fill it with garden soil.

4. Plant the herb in the bucket, water thoroughly, and then mulch in and around the bucket to conceal its edge.

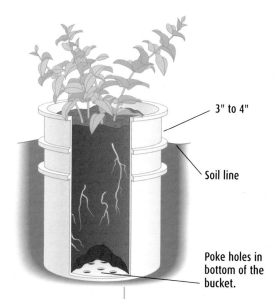

3" to 4"

Soil line

Poke holes in bottom of the bucket.

PREPARING PERENNIALS FOR WINTER

With the end of the growing season in sight and colder weather right around the corner, it's time to start putting the garden to bed for winter. The first thing to do is stop harvesting perennial herbs in late summer or early fall, about 3 weeks before you expect the first frost. Once frosts arrive and the ground has frozen, mulch heavily to protect perennials from winter heaving (when alternate freezing and thawing of the soil pushes plants right out of the ground). When mulching, keep these points in mind.

● Straw is the ideal winter mulch. (You don't want to use leaves because they might drift over the crowns of small plants and suffocate them.)

● Draw the mulch up to, but not over, the plants.

● Gray-leaved plants that hold their leaves over winter, such as lavender and thyme, need additional protection in cold climates. Laying evergreen boughs over the plants will help ensure their survival with minimal dieback.

Tender Perennials

Tender perennial herbs, such as bay and rosemary, need protection in most parts of the United States. In zones where they're not hardy, grow them in containers and bring them indoors over winter (see "Herbs in Containers" on page 32 for more on growing in containers). If you've been growing them in beds, you can still bring them indoors for the winter. Here's how.

1. Carefully dig up the plants and pot them.

2. Water the herbs and set them in a shady place outdoors for about a week, so they can gradually adjust to the dual shocks of pot culture and decreased sunlight. (If you're bringing herbs indoors that are already in pots, you'll still need to put them in shade for a week so they can adjust to the transition.)

3. Regularly check the plants, both outdoors and indoors, for pests such as whiteflies or aphids. If you find any, spray the plants with insecticidal soap.

Before the first frost, you need to bring any tender perennials indoors.

The best time to pot most outdoor herbs is after the fall harvest and before the first frost. They should be safely indoors by the time frost strikes. Chives, however, benefit from induced dormancy before coming in from the cold. Divide the clumps, pot them, and let them stay outside until frost kills the foliage. Then bring them in, and they'll give you a new burst of lush growth.

WINDOWSILL HERBS

Growing herbs indoors is a way to enjoy them all year long—particularly those herbs that wouldn't survive outdoors through the winter. No matter whether you decide to grow herbs as houseplants year-round or you're potting up perennials to move inside for the cold months, you'll give your plants an edge if you keep these points in mind.

Give them light. Most herbs thrive on at least 5 hours of sunlight a day. (Exceptions are the mints, parsley, rosemary, and thyme, which can take partial shade, and ginger and lemon balm, which actually like shade.)

Turn, turn, turn. Don't forget to turn the plants on windowsills regularly. Turning keeps them shapely and makes sure all sides get enough light.

When growing herbs indoors on your windowsill, make sure to water them and turn them regularly.

Keep it cool. Most herbs like temperatures on the cool side—daytime temps of 65°F and nighttime temps of 60°F.

Give them air. Herbs are extremely sensitive to dry, stagnant air—which is what you probably have in your tightly sealed, centrally heated house. Stale air promotes fungal diseases and insect infestations. So try to keep the air moving around the plants by cracking a window in an adjoining room or by opening doors. Also, don't crowd the pots—give them plenty of space so air can circulate around them.

Mix things up. Herbs in pots need a reasonably rich soil mix with good drainage, such as 2 parts compost, 1 part vermiculite, and 1 part perlite. Or, try a mix of 1 part potting soil, 1 part sand, and 1 part peat moss.

Water regularly. Although herbs enjoy regular waterings, they're finicky plants—meaning that they don't like waterlogged soil. Water most herbs thoroughly when the soil surface starts drying out. Let marjoram, oregano, sage, and thyme dry out between waterings. But never let rosemary completely dry out, or else you'll inadvertently kill it. And always use room temperature water so you don't shock the plants' root systems.

HERBS IN CONTAINERS

Herbs are great container plants, which means that you can grow them even if you don't have room for garden beds. Although potted herbs won't produce the big harvests you'd reap from garden-grown herbs, a few pots in a sunny site will produce plenty of fresh herbs and some to dry, as well. And growing tender herbs such as rosemary in pots makes it easy to move them indoors for the winter.

Care Basics

Containers. When choosing containers for herbs, select those that have drainage holes. Also, make sure the containers are large enough to allow 1 to 2 inches of space around the rootball. If the plants become rootbound, move them to larger containers.

quick tip

While growing herbs indoors is a great way to enjoy them year-round, some herbs are better suited for life within your home than others. Some of the best herbs for indoors include:

- Basil
- Chives
- Dill
- Ginger
- Marjoram
- Mints
- Oregano
- Parsley
- Rosemary
- Sage

Herbs look beautiful in containers, especially when they're combined with other plants.

Potting mix. A good, organic potting mix is important for container plants. See "Mix things up" on the opposite page for potting mix recipes you can make yourself.

Watering. You'll need to water herbs in containers more frequently than you would if they were growing in the garden. How often to water isn't rocket science, though. If you live where it's hot and dry, you'll need to water thoroughly and frequently. If you live where it's cool and wet, you'll need to water less often. (To check to see how moist the soil is, press your finger into the top inch of soil.)

Feeding. Herbs will benefit from a seasonal spray of liquid kelp or fish emulsion.

Air-drying herbs is an easy way to preserve your harvest.

chapter five

Harvesting Herbs

The payoff for growing herbs comes now—at harvesttime. Whether you snip a few leaves here and there to add zest to recipes or you cut bunches of herbs to store fresh, freeze, or dry, you'll savor having the convenience of delicious, garden-grown herbs at your fingertips all year long.

WHEN AND HOW TO HARVEST

To get the best harvest from your herbs, let your plants become established before you begin harvesting. Annual herbs, such as basil and dill, should be growing vigorously and have two or three pairs of true leaves. Don't take more than a few leaves from perennial herbs, such as chives or tarragon, the first year. Let them become established before doing any major harvesting.

Once your herbs are established and growing robustly, you can harvest continuously all season. Either snip leaves and blossoms as needed, or take larger harvests and preserve them for tasty winter dishes.

Let perennial herbs become established before doing any major harvesting.

How to Do It

For most herbs, cut just above a node when you harvest, to encourage new bushy growth. Chives and parsley are exceptions. To harvest chives, grab a handful of foliage and cut all the way through the bunch a few inches above the base. With parsley, harvest the outside stems first. When harvesting herb blossoms, leave several inches of stem attached. Also, if you're harvesting a lot of leaves because you want to preserve them, cut the stems; don't just strip off individual leaves and desert the unsightly naked stems in the garden.

quick tip

If you're growing herbs for their foliage, harvest leaves *before* the plants flower. Whether you plan on using them fresh, frozen, or dried, harvesting them before they flower will give you the best flavor. Choose healthy, tender foliage from the top of the plant. (Unless you've mulched, soil and debris accumulate on the lower leaves.)

Harvest foliage and edible flowers in the morning, just after the dew has dried. For the best-quality edible blossoms, such as chives, pick just before they're fully opened.

Ending the Season

Stop harvesting from perennial herbs a month or so before the first fall frost is expected, so the herb plants can store up the food reserves they need to weather the winter. Harvest annuals right up until frost.

STORING FRESH HERBS

To preserve the best flavor, aroma, and color, keep fresh herbs cool and dry after you harvest them (which means not washing the foliage and the blossoms unless absolutely necessary). If the leaves are gritty, swish bunches of herbs through a pan of ice water, then shake and pat them dry. Or, dig your salad spinner out of the back of the kitchen cabinet and use that to dry wet herbs.

You can store fresh herbs in the fridge in plastic bags or in water. Here's how.

● Put the herbs between paper towels, put the towels in resealable plastic bags, and then store the bags in the crisper drawer. Fresh herbs will last this way for 2 weeks or more.

If you want to store fresh herbs, like parsley, avoid washing them unless you absolutely have to.

- Set herb blossoms in a shallow bowl of water covered with plastic wrap. Kept cold, fresh blossoms will last up to 10 days.

FREEZING HERBS

Your freezer is one of the best places to preserve the homegrown flavor of herbs. You can freeze herbs individually or mix them together in special blends. For example, try combining basil, oregano, and thyme; or chives and dill. Most herbs will freeze well for up to 6 months if you freeze them just after harvesting.

You can freeze fresh herbs two ways.

- Chop the foliage with a sharp knife or scissors (use a food processor for large batches). Then pack the chopped herbs into resealable plastic bags. Squeeze air from the bags, seal them, and label them with the date and kind of herb. To use, just break off a piece and add it to the recipe—no thawing required!

- Puree the herb in a blender with water to liquefy, then pour the puree into ice cube trays and put the trays in your freezer. Once the cubes are frozen, pop them into labeled, resealable freezer bags.

DRYING HERBS

If you're looking for an easy way to preserve your herb harvest, drying is the way to go. You can dry herbs in any clean, dry, dark, dust-free, well-ventilated place. Dried herbs will keep their flavor for about a year.

Air Drying

Although attics are ideal places to air-dry herbs, any breezy room that you can keep dark will work. To air-dry herbs by hanging them, follow these steps.

1. Gather fresh herbs in small bunches. (Five or six stems per bunch is best; you can make larger bunches, but they won't dry as fast.)

quick tip

Unlike most other herbs, you should blanch basil before you freeze it, or it will turn black. To blanch, simply place the leaves in a strainer and pour boiling water over them for a second. Then lay the leaves on paper towels and let them cool naturally before freezing. Don't be tempted to cool the leaves by plunging them into ice water because this could dilute their flavor.

quick tip

You can also air-dry herbs on a screen in a clean, dry room. To make a simple drying screen, staple hardware cloth or window screening over a wooden frame. Strip leaves from their stems, then place the leaves in a single layer on the screens.

2. Secure the bunches of harvested herbs together with small rubber bands.

3. Hang the herbs upside down in a well-ventilated spot. Tie a paper bag over each bunch to keep light out and to catch pieces of herbs that fall off.

4. Check the bunches daily to see how they're coming along; they may take up to 2 weeks to dry.

5. When the leaves are completely dry and crisp, rub them off the stems and store them in jars out of the light. (Although storing them above or near your stove may seem to make the most sense, don't do it—the heat will dissipate their flavors.)

OVEN DRYING

You can dry herbs in your oven if you use very low heat. With a gas oven, simply leave the pilot light on—the oven temperature will be 85° to 90°F. Then spread a single layer of herbs on cookie sheets, and place the sheets on the oven racks. Stir the herbs once or twice; if you start in the morning, they should be dry by the end of the day. (You'll know they're finished drying when the leaves crumble as you rub them.)

When drying herbs in the oven, spread them out in a single layer on a cookie sheet.

If your oven is electric, turn it on its lowest setting and proceed as for gas; the herbs will dry in a matter of hours. (Oven drying works particularly well for succulent herbs like basil.)

MICROWAVE DRYING

A microwave is a great place to dry herbs because they retain excellent color and flavor when dried this way. Here's how to do it.

1. Lay the herb foliage in a single layer between two paper towels.

2. Microwave on high for 1 minute.

3. Check the herbs; if they're still soft, continue microwaving them for 20- to 30-second intervals.

4. The herbs are ready when they feel brittle and they rattle when you shake the paper towels or when the leaves pull easily from the stems.

Microwave drying is a bit easier on plant tissue than oven drying because the water in the herb leaves absorbs most of the heat. Once it heats up, it evaporates—that's why the paper towels get damp during the drying process—leaving drying plant tissue behind. The plant tissue heats up a little because of contact with the water, but the water absorbs most of the heat. In a conventional oven, all the plant material gets hot, not just the water.

DRYING WITH A DEHYDRATOR

A COMMERCIAL DEHYDRATOR is the ideal tool for drying herbs quickly. All you need to do is spread individual leaves or small sprigs of herbs, such as parsley, onto the trays, and turn the dehydrator on. In many cases, they'll dry overnight. You can also dry roots and thick stems in a commercial dryer. For faster drying, chop them into pieces first.

ANGELICA
(Angelica archangelica)

Angelica is a plant that stands out—literally—in any herb garden, as it can grow as high as 8 feet tall. This herb sort of looks like celery; it has a round, hollow stem that's purplish in color, and it has tiny white or greenish flowers. It's a biennial, or a short-lived perennial hardy in Zones 4 to 9.

Growing Guidelines

Rich, moist, well-drained soil and partial shade are the keys to making angelica happy. Plant the seeds directly in the ground in spring, but don't cover them, because they need light to germinate. Once the seedlings are up, thin them so they're about 3 feet apart.

After frost of the first year, angelica will die back to the ground. The following year it will send up new shoots that you can harvest in early spring. If you let the seedheads develop, the plant will die

Native to damp woodland meadows, angelica is an ideal choice for slightly shaded sites with moist soil.

IN THE KITCHEN

ANGELICA HAS A slightly sweet flavor. Although you can use the leaves to dress up green salads, fruit soups, or meat stews, the most celebrated part of angelica is its stem. Cook the stems like celery and eat them as a side dish or add them to stews. You can also candy the stem and savor it alone, or use it to decorate
- cakes - puddings - tarts

after the seed ripens—but you'll get replacement plants from the seeds that have self-sown.

Harvesting Hints

As mentioned earlier, you can harvest the stems (and leaves) in the spring of the second year of growth.

Trivia Tidbits

In ancient times, angelica was supposed to ward off evil spirits and witches. Peasants would make necklaces of the leaves for their children to wear for protection. And the juice of the roots was used to make a special drink thought to ensure a long life.

Angelica is the giant of the herb garden, reaching heights of up to 8 feet when in bloom.

A favorite of bees and butterflies, the purple spires of anise hyssop are equally attractive in the herb garden or the ornamental border.

ANISE HYSSOP
(Agastache foeniculum)

Anise hyssop is a sturdy and lovely plant that's as much at home in the perennial border as it is in the herb garden. The stems rise up to 3 feet tall and are topped with 3- to 6-inch spikes of lavender-blue flowers from midsummer to early autumn. You'll see a lot of bees and butterflies buzzing around this beauty, seeking its rich nectar. The leaves and flowers have a slight licoricelike scent and flavor. Anise hyssop is a perennial that grows in Zones 4 to 9.

Growing Guidelines

Although it prefers full sun, anise hyssop will also grow in light shade. A North American native, it's naturally found along lakeshores and streams in moist, well-drained soil that's very fertile.

You can buy young plants or start seeds indoors in late winter to transplant into the garden after the last spring frost—or you can sow the seeds directly in the

IN THE KITCHEN

FRESH LEAVES ARE excellent in salads. Or, chop them and add them to summer fruit cups, along with the colorful flowers. The licorice flavor of fresh minced leaves is also a nice complement to

● chicken ● fish ● pork ● rice

Fresh and dried leaves make a good tea, alone or in combination with other herbs.

garden a week before the last expected frost. Space seeds about 1 to 1½ feet apart. Even though anise hyssop is a perennial, the seedlings will usually reach blooming size the first year.

After a hard frost, the plants will die back to the ground. Be sure you mark the location of your plants, as they are very slow to emerge in the spring.

Plants do tend to be short-lived, so divide the clumps every year or two in spring to keep them vigorous. Even if the parent plants die out, you'll generally have plenty of self-sown volunteers to replace them.

Harvesting Hints

For occasional use, snip off the leaves as needed, starting from the bottom of the plant.

The fresh flowers are attractive in salads and make a nice addition to potpourri. Cut them just as they begin to open.

For tea, cut the whole stems 4 to 5 inches from the base of the plant and strip the leaves off. To air-dry whole stems, gather them early in the day and hang them in a well-ventilated, dark, dry location.

Trivia Tidbits

The botanical name, *Agastache foeniculum*, refers to the many flower spikes on this fennel-like plant. It is just one of many unrelated plants that share the anise scent that is characteristic of fennel.

The Cheyenne called this herb "Elk-Mint" and made infusions of the leaves.

Anise hyssop has heart-shaped leaves with a delicate licorice flavor. Enjoy them by themselves or mixed with mints and lemon balm in iced summer teas and hot winter brews.

BASIL
(*Ocimum basilicum*)

Basil's pungent flavor enhances any summer garden recipe. And you can choose from lots of varieties, including lemon, cinnamon, and anise-flavored types. Basil also comes in a variety of shapes and colors; you can plant varieties that are low-growing, stocky, or tall, with variegated, crinkled, purple, green, or smooth leaves. Basil is an annual that will grow in Zones 4 through 10. The plants can grow up to 2 feet tall and 8 inches wide.

Basil is available in a tantalizing variety of flavors. Find the ones you love and plant them near the kitchen so they'll be close at hand when you're making salads and sauces.

IN THE KITCHEN

BASIL HAS A rich and spicy, mildly peppery flavor, with a trace of mint and clove. For the best flavor, use basil fresh, rather than dried. Traditional in Italian, Mediterranean, and Thai cooking, basil is superb with

- tomatoes
- white beans
- pasta
- rice
- cheese
- eggs
- fish
- lamb
- poultry
- veal

You can also pair basil with a host of mild vegetables, such as zucchini, summer squash, and eggplant. If you make your own pizza or tomato sauce, try substituting basil for oregano and see how you like the taste.

Growing Guidelines

You can grow basil in any well-drained soil amended with plenty of organic matter. Just make sure you plant basil where it will get full sun.

Start basil seeds indoors 6 weeks before your last expected frost. Plant the transplants outdoors after the danger of frost has passed and when soil temperature averages 50°F or higher. If you're growing small-leaved basil, place the plants 6 to 8 inches apart. Varieties with large leaves need 1 to 1½ feet between plants.

Mulching the area after the seedlings have shot up helps to keep the ground moist and warm and discourages weeds. But make sure you mulch *after* the ground has warmed up because basil roots need heat.

Harvesting Hints

Begin harvesting basil as soon as the plants have several pairs of leaves. If you harvest frequently, you'll help encourage your plants to produce new growth— which, in turn, will give you even more basil to harvest. You can keep harvesting basil up until the first frost. After harvesting, wrap dry foliage in paper towels and store it in resealable plastic bags in the fridge.

Trivia Tidbits

In Italy, basil has been and still is a sign of love. According to tradition, if a man gives a woman a sprig of basil, she will fall in love with him and never leave him. Today, he'd probably have better luck if he made her pesto and served it over pasta with salad, bread, and a little wine—and then did the dishes afterward.

Purple basils like 'Red Rubin' provide a striking accent in the herb garden. Infuse white wine vinegar with their pungent leaves, and it will turn a beautiful amethyst color.

Starry blue borage flowers taste like cucumber and make a beautiful and tasty addition to salads.

BORAGE
(Borage officinalis)

Borage produces blue, star-shaped blossoms and is a nice addition to a wildflower bed or vegetable patch, as well as to your herb garden. This annual, which can grow up to 2 feet tall and 16 inches wide, attracts lots of bees, which love its flowers.

Growing Guidelines

Borage needs fairly rich, moist, light soil and full sun to grow. This herb is easy to grow from seed. Plant the seed as soon as the danger of frost has passed. (Borage will

IN THE **KITCHEN**

BORAGE HAS A crisp cucumber flavor. You can use the leaves raw, steamed, or sautéed, as you would spinach. You can eat the flowers and stems, too; peel, chop, and use the stems like celery. The leaves and stems enhance

- most vegetables
- green salads
- salad dressings
- pickles
- cheese
- fish
- poultry
- iced beverages

Borage also blends well with dill, mint, and garlic. If you don't care for the fuzziness of borage leaves, simply use them for flavor only and take them out of the food before you serve it.

readily reseed itself after its initial planting.) When the seedlings poke their heads through the ground, thin them so they're about 2 feet apart.

Because borage likes moist soil, mulch around the plants to help contain moisture. Don't be disappointed if the pretty blue flowers don't appear on your new plants the first year; sometimes borage acts as a biennial.

Harvesting Hints

Harvest borage as you need it for fresh use, gathering the young, tender leaves in the morning, after the dew has dried. Always use borage fresh because it loses its flavor and color when dried.

Trivia Tidbits

Borage has a reputation for invoking courage. In fact, ancient Celtic warriors preparing for battle drank wine flavored with borage to give them courage. They believed their fears would vanish and they would feel elated. (The effect was probably due to the wine, not the borage.)

Once established, borage is an exuberant grower and self-seeds readily. Transplant errant seedlings while they're small to avoid damaging their roots.

While cats revel in the scent of catnip, the leaves make a calming tea for humans.

CATNIP
(Nepeta cataria)

Catnip, which many people plant for their cat's enjoyment, is a member of the mint family. Cats love this feline drug, sniffing, chewing, and rolling around in it. (Humans, on the other hand, can only feel envy at all the feline fun.) Actually, smelling catnip—not eating it—is what does the trick for cats. A happy cat may chew on the plant, but that's mostly to bruise it and release more of the magic fragrance.

Catnip is coarse-leaved and gray-green, and it produces white flowers with purple-pink spots. A perennial, catnip can grow 1 to 3 feet tall and is hardy to Zone 3 or 4.

Growing Guidelines

Catnip does best in average, sandy, well-drained soil, in an area that gets full sun to partial shade (although it will be most fragrant if you plant it in full sun). The easiest way to start a catnip patch is by planting a whole plant (check out your local garden center or ask a friend with an established patch if she has any extra plants).

FUN FACT

CATNIP CAME TO AMERICA ALONG WITH OTHER NECESSITIES FOR PIONEER LIVING. AMERICA'S FIRST GEOGRAPHER LISTED IT IN 1796 AS A COMMERCIAL CROP. IT ESCAPED CULTIVATION AND INVADED THE LANDSCAPE. IT EVEN WORKED ITS WAY INTO AMERICAN LITERATURE, APPEARING IN THE WRITINGS OF WASHINGTON IRVING, NATHANIEL HAWTHORNE, AND HARRIET BEECHER STOWE.

Harvesting Hints

Gather the leaves and tops in late summer when the plant is in full bloom, and dry them in the shade. Store dried leaves away from moisture.

Healing with Catnip

Some people make a tea from the dried leaves and flowering heads as a remedy for upset stomachs and insomnia.

Trivia Tidbits

During the Middle Ages, catnip was thought—incorrectly—to prevent leprosy.

If it's a low-maintenance herb you're looking for, plant catnip! It grows happily in the most ordinary garden soils, requiring almost no care.

German chamomile is an annual herb easily grown from seed. Harvest the tiny, daisylike flowers to make a relaxing bedtime tea.

CHAMOMILE, GERMAN
(*Matricaria recutita*)

CHAMOMILE, ROMAN
(*Chamaemelum nobile*)

Although you're probably familiar with the word chamomile, you may not know that it's two different plants. German chamomile is an annual reaching 2 to 3 feet tall. It has a honey-apple fragrance and is the chamomile commonly found in tea bags. Roman chamomile is a low-growing perennial that rarely reaches more than 9 inches high—making it suitable for use as a groundcover. It's hardy in Zones 6 to 9 and normally carries a stronger fragrance than its German counterpart.

Growing Guidelines

German chamomile prefers sandy, well-drained soil, while Roman chamomile does best in light, dry soil. Plant both types in full sun to partial shade.

You can sow chamomile seeds outdoors in early spring or late summer by scattering them where you want them to grow in the garden. Don't cover the seeds with soil, though, because they need light to germinate. Keep the soil evenly moist (not soggy).

quick tip

Tired after a stressful day at work? Try a soothing chamomile bath. Just steep a couple handfuls of chamomile in water for 15 minutes, let it cool, and pour it into your bathwater. (You can also use it as a skin lotion.)

Or try a chamomile facial. Simply place some dried chamomile flowers in a large bowl, pour boiling water over the flowers, then let the steam waft over your face.

When the seedlings are 1 to 2 inches tall, thin them so that they're 8 to 12 inches apart. (For a groundcover, thin Roman chamomile seedlings to 4 inches apart.)

Harvesting Hints

If you're going to use chamomile for tea, harvest the flowers in full bloom throughout the summer. Spread the flowers thinly on a cloth or screen to dry in the shade. Throw away any stem or leaf parts, and store the flowers in an airtight container away from heat, light, and moisture.

Healing with Chamomile

Chamomile tea helps alleviate insomnia and calm nerves. It also relieves indigestion, nausea, and flatulence. A gargle with cooled tea helps relieve mouth inflammations and sore throats.

Trivia Tidbits

In the days before refrigeration, immersing meat in chamomile tea was thought to help eliminate the rancid odor of spoilage. Chamomile was also reputed to make an excellent insect repellent. And the fresh, delicate fragrance of this daisylike herb made it a popular air freshener in homes where bathing was uncommon.

Grow perennial Roman chamomile along the pathways in your garden so you can enjoy its fruity fragrance anytime you step on or brush against its foliage.

Chervil's tiny white flowers are a favorite nectar source of parasitic wasps and other beneficial insects.

CHERVIL
(Anthriscus cerefolium)

Chervil comes in two main varieties, one plain and one curly. A hardy annual, chervil looks dainty and delicate and produces small white flowers on plants that can grow to 2 feet tall.

Growing Guidelines

Chervil likes a rich, humusy, slightly acid soil. Plant it in early spring or fall, since it prefers cool temperatures and bolts (goes to seed) at the first sign of heat. You can direct-seed chervil

IN THE KITCHEN

CHERVIL HAS A subtle, tender flavor—part anise, part parsley—and is an effective seasoning in food. You can use both the leaves and the stems in cooking, and whole sprigs make a delicate and decorative garnish. Chervil enhances

- carrots
- corn
- peas
- spinach
- eggs
- cream
- veal
- fish and seafood (especially oysters)

Chervil also complements tarragon, shallots, freshly ground black pepper, marjoram, and lemon. Always add chervil at the end of cooking because lengthy heating turns the flavor bitter.

shallowly in the ground. When the seedlings reach 2 inches high, thin them to 9 to 12 inches apart.

Keep mulch away from the bases of the plants, or they may be damaged by earwigs. Also, cover small seedlings with floating row covers to protect them from rabbits, groundhogs, or other animal pests.

Harvesting Hints

Snip the feathery leaves 6 to 8 weeks after sowing. Use chervil fresh because dried leaves have little flavor.

Trivia Tidbits

Chervil's flavor and fragrance resemble that of the myrrh brought by the wise men to the baby Jesus. Because of this and because chervil symbolized new life, it became traditional to serve chervil soup on Holy Thursday.

Chervil self-seeds readily. The bright green leaves appear early in spring to herald the up-coming growing season.

No garden should be without at least one clump of chives. Their mildly onion-flavored leaves accent everything from potatoes and fish to salads and corn.

CHIVES
(Allium schoenoprasum)

Chives are bulb plants, although the bulbs are so tiny that you might not realize they're there. These plants produce beautiful, globelike, pink and lavender blossoms. A perennial, chives grow to about 18 inches high and thrive in Zones 3 to 9.

Growing Guidelines

This herb requires well-drained soil and full sun. The easiest way to grow chives is to start with young plants

IN THE KITCHEN

CHIVES TASTE LIKE mild, sweet onions. Mince the fresh, slender leaves, and use them in recipes or as a garnish. French cooking combines chives with shallots, marjoram, and tarragon. Chives also complement

- artichokes
- asparagus
- carrots
- cauliflower
- corn
- onions
- peas
- potatoes
- spinach
- tomatoes
- cheese
- eggs
- fish and shellfish
- poultry

Don't overlook chive flowers, either. Toss them in salads or add them to a dish as a beautiful, edible garnish.

acquired from garden centers, by mail order, or from a friend. Plant clumps of up to six chive bulbs 5 to 8 inches apart.

Keep mulch away from the bases of the plants to improve air circulation and prevent disease problems. Chives compete poorly with other plants, so make sure to weed diligently.

You'll need to divide large clumps of chives about every 3 years. In early spring, dig up the plants and work the clumps apart with your fingers to create small clumps of four to six bulbs each. Then replant these divisions (or share them with friends).

Harvesting Hints

Use scissors to cut chives about 2 inches above the soil. Before the plants flower in spring, harvest from the outside edges of the clumps. After the plants flower, cut back the entire plant to remove the spent flowerstalks. Chives are best if you use them fresh.

Chive's purple pom-pom flowers are edible, too. Break them apart and toss them on top of salads, or tie them into bundles and use them as a garnish.

Trivia Tidbits

Chives have been added to foods for nearly 5,000 years. Native to the Orient, they were probably first used by the Chinese and then the ancient Greeks. By the sixteenth century, they had also earned a place in European herb gardens. When the colonists came to America, they brought chives along with them.

Coriander or cilantro? It's both! The pungent leaves are called cilantro, and the seeds that appear after it flowers are known as coriander.

CORIANDER
(Coriandrum sativum)

People have used coriander in cooking since ancient times. This cool-weather annual has pale mauve flowers that bees and other pollinators just love. (The flowers appear in spring or mid- to late summer, depending on when you sow them.) Those flowers produce seedpods that are harvested for the spice coriander. The lower leaves of the plant, commonly called cilantro, are round with slightly scalloped edges. Coriander grows 2 to 3 feet tall.

IN THE KITCHEN

CORIANDER LEAVES HAVE a bold taste that combines a strong sage flavor with a sharp hint of citrus. You can mince the fresh leaves and add them to foods such as salsa, or you can use them whole as a lacy garnish.

Coriander seeds are sweetly aromatic, with a slight hint of citrus. Whole or ground seeds add character to

- salad dressings
- marinades
- chili sauce
- cheese
- guacamole
- eggs

The flavor of coriander also combines nicely with beets, onions, potatoes, clams, oysters, and sausage.

Growing Guidelines

Coriander prefers sunny sites with well-drained soil. Sow the seeds directly in the garden about ½ inch deep after the danger of frost has passed. After the seedlings appear, thin them to 4 inches apart and keep them evenly moist. Make sure you don't over-fertilize this herb because too much nitrogen in the soil will produce a less-flavorful plant.

Harvesting Hints

Harvest fresh coriander leaves as needed. Coriander seeds ripen and scatter quickly, so cut the entire plant as soon as the leaves and flowers turn brown. Tie the plants in bundles, and hang them upside down with a paper bag tied securely around the flowerheads to catch the seeds as they dry.

Although cilantro pairs perfectly with heat lovers like tomatoes and peppers in the kitchen, outside in the garden, high temperatures will quickly send it to seed. Keep the green leaves coming by planting varieties like 'Slow-bolt', or plan for a late-summer or early-fall crop.

Trivia Tidbits

Greek and Roman doctors, including Hippocrates, made medicines from coriander, but it was also prized as a spice and as an ingredient in a Roman vinegar used to preserve meat. The Chinese used coriander as far back as the Han dynasty—207 B.C. to A.D. 220. At the time, it was thought that coriander had the power to make a person immortal.

Who can imagine a jar of Grandma's crunchy pickles without a lacy yellow dill flower floating in the brine?

DILL
(Anethum graveolens)

Dill is simple to grow and beautiful to look at, which is why you should add it to your garden. This annual herb grows in Zones 2 through 9 and looks like a smaller version of fennel, its relative. Dill can grow up to 3 feet tall and has pretty yellow flowers and feathery, blue-green leaves.

Growing Guidelines

Dill needs moist soil with good drainage and full sun. This herb doesn't transplant well, so you'll have the best luck if

IN THE KITCHEN

DILL HAS A pickle flavor. You can use its feathery leaves fresh in salads and as garnishes; use the seeds whole or ground in longer-cooking recipes. Dill is delicious paired with fish (especially salmon), as well as

- cabbage
- cucumbers
- potatoes
- cheese
- cream
- eggs
- lamb
- pork
- poultry

Dillweed is easiest to handle when it's frozen on its stem. Simply snip some off with scissors as needed, and put the rest back in the freezer.

you sow the seeds directly in the ground in spring, after the danger of frost has passed. (Make sure to weed diligently because small dill seedlings don't compete well against other plants.) When the seedlings are about 2 inches high, thin them so they're 10 to 12 inches apart. If you're growing dill mostly for the foliage, you can sow the seeds just 8 to 10 inches apart; do so every 3 weeks for a constant supply of dillweed.

If you're growing dill for the seeds, keep in mind that seeds may not be produced until the beginning of the plant's second year.

Harvesting Hints

Once the plants are well established (about 8 to 10 weeks after sowing), you can begin clipping the leaves close to the stem. You'll have to use it soon because dillweed will last only a couple of days in the refrigerator before it droops and loses its flavor. Or, you can freeze the freshly picked leaves.

Harvest the seeds when the flower matures, anywhere from 2 to 3 weeks after blossoming (the seeds will be a light brown color). When you cut the stems, make sure you leave enough of the stem on so that you can tie the plants into a bunch and hang them in a dark place for drying.

Trivia Tidbits

The name dill comes from dilla, Norse for "to lull." Dill was believed to work as a charm against witches; mystics could combat an "evil eye" spell by carrying a bag of dried dill over the heart.

Dill is easy to grow from seed sown directly in the garden. You'll find that your home-grown leaves are far more flavorful than the ones sold in supermarkets.

Florence fennel or "finocchio" (Foeniculum vulgare var. azoricum) produces a bulbous stalk that tastes delicious when braised whole or shredded into fresh salads.

FENNEL

(*Foeniculum vulgare*)

Fennel's filigreed leaves and small yellow flowers dance in the wind. This herb stands tall (about 4 feet high) to make a good border, or, when intermittently placed among shorter specimens, creates an unusual garden skyline. Fennel is a semihardy perennial, but most people grow it as an annual. It will grow in Zones 6 through 9.

Growing Guidelines

You can plant fennel seeds directly in the ground as soon as you can work the soil in spring. Plant the seeds

IN THE KITCHEN

IF YOU LIKE the taste of licorice, then fennel is for you. Use fresh leaves in salads and as lacy garnishes; you can eat the tender stems like celery. Use the seeds, whole or ground, to dress up breads, cakes, and cookies. Fennel also goes well with

- beets
- rice
- potatoes
- eggs
- pickles
- cheese
- barley
- fish

The leaves and seeds lend aroma and flavor to herb butters, cheese spreads, and salad dressings.

about 6 inches apart in a rich, well-drained bed that gets full sun. (Make sure to plant fennel away from coriander, which will prevent fennel's seeds from forming.) Cover the seeds shallowly and keep the soil moist. For a continuous crop of fennel during the growing season, keep planting seeds every 2 to 3 weeks. (**Note:** One or two plants will probably produce plenty of leaves for your family so you may want to succession sow only if you're growing extra for friends.)

Harvesting Hints

Begin snipping the leaves once the plant is well established—about 8 to 10 weeks after planting the seed. Then just keep harvesting the leaves as you need them.

If you want to harvest the seeds, you'll need to keep a close eye on the plants so you'll notice when the seeds turn from yellowish green to brown. When that happens, use scissors to snip the entire seedhead and let it drop into a paper bag. Store the bag in a warm, dark place for further drying. Once the seeds are thoroughly dried, store them in glass jars.

Once it gets a foothold, fennel will self-seed with abandon. Keep it within bounds by clipping off the flowers before the seedheads have a chance to shatter.

Trivia Tidbits

In medieval times, people kept a stash of fennel seeds handy to nibble on through long church services and on fast days; the seeds were considered to be an appetite suppressant.

If you simply remember to cut off the spent flowers, feverfew will supply you with a profusion of daisylike flowers throughout the summer.

FEVERFEW
(Chrysanthemum parthenium)

A member of the daisy family, feverfew sports small, white flowers with yellow centers. This herb looks similar to chamomile; you can tell them apart because feverfew stands up straight, while chamomile tends to bend over. Feverfew is a short-lived perennial that's often grown as an annual. It grows 2 to 3 feet tall—making it perfect for defining garden borders—and is hardy in Zones 4 to 9.

Growing Guidelines

Feverfew prefers full sun and well-drained soil. In spring, after the danger of frost has passed, sow the seeds by scattering them on top of prepared soil and lightly raking them in. Once the seedlings have germinated (they do so pretty quickly), thin them to 12 inches apart. (Be on guard, though—feverfew is a profuse self-seeder and may spread beyond your garden.)

Harvesting Hints

Harvest feverfew's leaves before the plant blooms in summer. Pinch back or shear off the tops of the stems. Dry the leaves by spreading them in a single layer on a cloth or screen in the shade. Store dried leaves in an airtight container away from heat and light.

quick tip

You can use low-growing varieties of feverfew as annuals in rock gardens, window boxes, and in containers for summer and fall blooming. You can also dry the stems of feverfew to add to herb and flower arrangements.

Healing with Feverfew

True to its name, feverfew reduces fevers (its common name comes from the Latin word *febrifugia*, or "fever reducer") and is a mild sedative. Modern research has also shown that the regular use of feverfew reduces the frequency and severity of migraines and associated symptoms, such as nausea and vomiting. In addition, the herb's anti-inflammatory qualities may provide relief to arthritis sufferers.

Trivia Tidbits

In its long history, this herb has been used as an ingredient in making sweets and wines; as an aromatic to ward off disease; and as an insect repellent. It was also used to treat infant colic, vertigo, arthritis, kidney stones, and constipation.

Feverfew will happily fill in empty areas in herb gardens or ornamental borders.

GARLIC
(*Allium sativum*)

Garlic's aromatic bulbs are a seasoning and a vegetable in one. Softneck types have tops that flop over as they dry, so they're best for braiding. Hardneck garlic has a stiff, upright flowerstalk (which can grow to 2 feet high). All types of garlic are perennials grown as annuals.

Growing Guidelines

Plant garlic in full sun in well-drained soil. You can plant in midfall or early spring as soon as the soil is workable. Although you can start garlic from bulbils, it's much faster and easier to plant cloves.

Set the cloves with the root end (the wider end) 1 to 2 inches deep, 6 to 8 inches apart. (If you're planting in fall, the cloves will produce shoots immediately, then become dormant until spring.) In spring, side-dress the plants with compost. Keep the soil evenly moist until the tops begin to die, then stop watering so the bulbs can mature.

A few rows of garlic cloves tucked into the soil in fall will reward you with an early burst of green growth the following spring.

IN THE KITCHEN

GARLIC HAS A strong, oniony taste that livens up tomato sauce and pesto. (You can soften garlic's flavor by using it in recipes that require long, moist cooking, like stewing.) Other foods that are enhanced by garlic include

- cheese spreads
- herb butters
- herb vinegars
- pickles
- meat
- poultry

Harvesting Hints

Eventually, the tops of the garlic plants will begin to bend and turn brown. Garlic is ready to harvest when most (about 75 percent) of the leaves have turned brown. Pull fall-planted garlic in late June or early July; pull spring-planted garlic at the end of the season. Use a digging fork to lift garlic from the soil. Lay the whole plants in an airy, dark, dry spot for several weeks to cure. Then trim away leaves and brush off dirt.

Garlic keeps best if you store the bulbs in a cool, dark, dry spot.

Trivia Tidbits

The Romans took garlic to strengthen them in battle because it was the "herb of Mars." (Mars was the Roman god of war.) European legend says that if a man chews on a garlic bulb during a footrace, no one will be able to get ahead of him. (And it's doubtful anyone would even want to draw close!)

Rocambole, also called hard-neck garlic, produces bulbs with large, meaty cloves that are easy to break apart and peel.

Plant versatile lavender to lend a hint of the Mediterranean to herb beds, shrub borders, or rock gardens.

LAVENDER
(*Lavandula angustifolia*)

Lavender has a classic fragrance that's reminiscent of days gone by—or at least of your grandma's house, where she had lavender sachets tucked into drawers. But despite its old-fashioned connotations, this perennial herb (it's hardy in Zones 5 to 8) is still quite popular today. And with good reason: Lavender smells great, works well in any garden setting (it can grow up to 30 inches tall), and has a myriad of uses.

Growing Guidelines

This herb needs a sunny site with excellent drainage. (If your soil isn't well drained, you can amend it with compost and coarse gravel.) Lavender is difficult to start from seed because it needs a long time to germinate. So ask friends for cuttings or buy plants from your local garden center or from a mail-order supplier. Place plants 2 feet apart and water regularly for the next few weeks. Once established, though, lavender is very drought tolerant.

If you live in Zone 7 or colder, protect your lavender plants with a winter mulch of evergreen boughs to ensure strong new growth the following spring.

As it grows, lavender's stems can become woody. Keep your lavender looking its best by pruning it back by about half its height every 2 or 3 years in spring.

FUN FACT

In the Middle Ages, lavender was thought to be an herb of love; however, a sprinkle of lavender water on a person's head was thought to keep that person chaste.

Harvesting Hints

If you're planning on drying lavender, harvest the flowers either when they first open or when they're full. To dry the flowers, spread them flat on paper or hang them in bunches in a warm, dry place, like an attic. Well-dried lavender flowers will remain aromatic for a long time.

Healing with Lavender

In France and Spain, bruises and bites are treated with lavender compresses, while compresses of warm lavender tea are thought to relieve chest congestion.

Trivia Tidbits

Up until World War I, lavender was used as a disinfectant for wounds.

Slip a few sprigs of lavender into your dresser drawers to infuse lingerie and linens with old-fashioned fragrance.

Be sure to make some room in your herb garden for lemon balm. Its lemon-scented leaves add a citrusy zing to teas and punches.

LEMON BALM
(Melissa officinalis)

Brush this perennial herb's leaves and your fingers will smell of lemon with a hint of mint. Hardy in Zones 5 to 9, lemon balm produces tiny white or light blue flowers (much loved by bees) in May or June. The flowers bloom throughout the summer, and the plant grows to about 2 feet high.

Growing Guidelines

Lemon balm isn't particular about soil or site (in fact, it can become invasive if left unattended). It prefers average soil in full sun, but will make do in partial shade. Sow seed directly in the ground about 12 to 24 inches apart in

IN THE KITCHEN

FRESH LEMON BALM leaves make a relaxing hot tea; you can also toss a few sprigs of lemon balm into cool summer punches or iced tea. In addition to beverages, toss whole or chopped fresh leaves into

- green salads
- marinated vegetables
- fruit salads
- poultry stuffing

Lemon balm also teams well with asparagus, beans, broccoli, corn, freshly ground black pepper, olives, lamb, and shellfish.

early spring or fall. When the plant becomes over-grown, dig up and divide the roots, then replant the divisions in either spring or fall.

Harvesting Hints

If you want to use lemon balm immediately, pick the leaves at their peak of flavor and fragrance. For later use, harvest the leaves just before the plants begin to bloom, tie the stems in small bundles, and hang them in an airy spot out of direct sunlight to dry.

Trivia Tidbits

The Greek physician Dioscorides put lemon balm on scorpion and dog bites, and then he would drop some more into wine for the patient to drink. And bee-keepers used to rub lemon balm inside a hive to encourage a new swarm to stay.

Lemon balm grows with the carefree abandon typical of its mint-family relatives. Pull out rampant seedlings before they have a chance to mingle too far into the rest of the garden.

Keep a pot of lemon verbena growing on your windowsill and you'll be able to enjoy its intensely fragrant leaves all year long.

LEMON VERBENA
(*Aloysia triphylla*)

Lemon verbena is a deciduous woody shrub that has tiny lavender flowers and attractive foliage. Simply brush by this plant and you'll release its sweet, lemony fragrance. It's only hardy in Zones 9 and 10, but it works well as a container plant—which means you can still grow it if you live where winters are cold; you just have to bring it indoors. Lemon verbena grows 10 to 15 feet high outdoors in warm climates and up to 5 feet high in cooler climates or indoors. It flowers in late summer and fall.

IN THE KITCHEN

LEMON VERBENA IS most often used to make a delicately flavored tea. You can also use this herb wherever you want to add a touch of lemon, such as in rice, pound cake, or zucchini bread. Fresh or dried leaves also brighten the taste of

- vegetable marinades
- salad dressings
- fish
- poultry
- jams
- puddings
- beverages

Fresh lemon verbena leaves are tough, though, so be sure to remove them from marinades, beverages, and salad dressings before serving.

Growing Guidelines

Unless you live in a very mild climate, you'll probably grow lemon verbena in a container. This plant does best in rich, moist (but not soggy) soil and full sun. Lemon verbena also likes a lot of nutrients, so feed your plant regularly with fish emulsion. (Remember: This herb is deciduous, so don't be concerned when it loses its leaves in fall.) Cut the plant back halfway in midsummer and again in the beginning of fall to keep it bushy.

You can take your container-grown lemon verbena outdoors during the warmer months. If you choose to expose your plant to the good life outside, make sure you place the container on top of a hard surface, such as tile or bricks. That way, the roots won't escape from the pot and take hold in the ground.

You can propagate new lemon verbena plants from stem cuttings taken in mid- to late summer. Root the cuttings in a moist mixture of equal parts sand and peat moss.

Harvesting Hints

You can harvest sprigs of lemon verbena leaves almost all year long.

Trivia Tidbits

Lemon verbena hasn't figured as an important medicinal herb, probably in part due to its late introduction to Europe (it's native to Chile and Argentina). It has, however, been used in folk medicine to aid digestion and to reduce fevers.

A sprig of lovage will add a burst of flavor to even the most ordinary winter stews.

LOVAGE
(Levisticum officinale)

This perennial herb tastes like celery, but is a lot easier to grow. The plant can reach 5 feet tall, making it a large, dramatic specimen for your garden. Another plus for lovage is its cold tolerance; it's hardy to Zone 3.

Growing Guidelines

Lovage does best in moist, fertile, well-drained soil in a site that receives full sun to partial shade. Since you'll probably only want one lovage plant,

IN THE KITCHEN

AS MENTIONED ABOVE, lovage leaves, stems, and seeds all taste like celery. You can use the leaves fresh in salads and fresh or dried in soups, stews, and sauces. Chop and add the stems to salads; you can also cook and puree them. The seeds, whole or ground, work well in pickling brines, cheese spreads, salads, salad dressings, and sauces.

Lovage also enhances

- potatoes (especially potato salad)
- tomatoes
- steamed vegetables
- rice
- chicken
- poultry stuffings

purchase a seedling from your local nursery or ask a friend for a cutting. Whether you use seedlings or divisions, set them at least 2 feet apart. Wait 2 years before harvesting the roots or stems. Also, side-dress plants with a rich compost each spring, and keep them well watered during dry spells.

Harvesting Hints

Gather seeds when the tiny fruits begin to open, which means they're ripe.

Cut the leaves or stems whenever you want to use them. To dry leaves and stems, hang them upside down in a warm, shady spot, like an attic. When dry, store the leaves and stems in tightly sealed, opaque containers because light will quickly yellow this herb.

Trivia Tidbits

Lovage was very popular in the Middle Ages, when people grew it in kitchen gardens. Early herbalists recommended lovage as a diuretic, and occasionally as a cure for rheumatism, jaundice, malaria, sore throats, and kidney stones.

Lovage is much easier to grow than its flavor counterpart, celery, and its flavor is even more concentrated, so you'll need a lot less.

Sweet marjoram is a pretty yet tough little plant that makes a great groundcover. The leaves taste great in soups and sauces, too!

MARJORAM
(Origanum majorana)

Marjoram is a gentle, subtly perfumed, calming herb whose fragrance livens recipes, potpourris, and other crafts. A tender perennial, marjoram will overwinter in Zones 9 and 10, but it is usually grown as an annual. It grows to about 1 foot tall.

Growing Guidelines

This herb prefers full sun and light, well-drained soil. Because marjoram seeds are small and slow to germinate, you'll need to start them indoors 6 to 8 weeks before your last expected spring frost. When you

IN THE KITCHEN

Marjoram tastes something like a mild oregano, with a hint of balsam. This herb is especially good with beef, roast poultry, green vegetables, eggs, potatoes, squash, and tomatoes. You can also add it to

- stews
- marinades
- dressings
- herb butters
- cheese spreads
- soups
- stuffings
- flavored vinegars and oils

Experiment and pair marjoram with other herbs, too. It complements basil, bay, garlic, onion, and thyme.

transplant the plants to the garden, space them about 8 inches apart.

In the fall, dig plants and transfer them to containers for winter harvest indoors. Replant them again in spring.

Harvesting Hints

Begin harvesting marjoram 5 to 6 weeks after transplanting into your garden, or when the plants are growing vigorously. You can keep harvesting marjoram to use fresh as you need it. You might also want to dry some; unlike some other herbs, marjoram retains a lot of its flavor when dried. Dry it away from sunlight to preserve both color and flavor. When dried, rub the stems on a screen to shred the leaves, discard the stems, and store the shredded leaves in airtight containers.

Trivia Tidbits

The Greeks called marjoram "joy of the mountains" and used it at weddings and funerals and to cure rheumatism.

Invite pollinators to lunch! Sweet marjoram is long-flowering, providing pollinating insects with an alternate source of nectar when other crops aren't in bloom.

Spearmint, peppermint, lemon mint, and more! Grow several types of mint and have fun comparing flavors.

MINTS
(Mentha spp.)

Mint seems to be a good antidote to hot summer days, when you need something cool and refreshing from your garden. And when it comes to growing mint, you have a lot of flavors to choose from: apple, lemon, orange, pineapple, peppermint, and spearmint, to name just a few. Most mints are tough perennials, so they're easy herbs for beginners. They'll grow in Zones 5 to 9, and can reach up to 2 feet high.

Growing Guidelines

Plant mints in full sun or partial shade in rich, moist, well-drained soil. Mint often doesn't come true from seed, so ask a friend for cuttings or visit your local garden center for seedlings.

Although mint is an easy herb to grow, it can spread aggressively—and then you'll have a difficult time getting rid of it. To prevent mint from spreading, plant it in 5-gallon containers with holes punched in the bottom for drainage.

Frequent cutting will keep mints at their prettiest. It encourages stems to branch out and makes for lusher,

quick tip

Here's how to make a refreshing glass of mint water: Crush 1 cup of peppermint, spearmint, or other mint. Place the mint in a clean, ½-gallon container and fill it with fresh, cool water. Chill the container in your refrigerator for a couple of hours. Then strain the leaves out, and serve the mint water over ice.

healthier plants. In late fall, after your final harvest, cut your mint plants to the ground. This eliminates overwintering sites for mint pests, such as spider mites and aphids.

Harvesting Hints

Fresh is best when it comes to mint. And because mint is such a tough plant, you can start harvesting it almost as soon as it comes up in spring. Harvest heavily and continuously to encourage new growth, then stop harvesting 2 to 4 weeks before fall frosts.

Healing with Mint

Of all the mints, peppermint is the one that has the most medicinal effects. You can use it to calm an upset stomach or relieve gas. Peppermint may also help relieve menstrual cramps.

Trivia Tidbits

Beginning in the eighteenth century, mint became an important medicinal herb. Japanese mint was thought to aid fertility, while a remedy for mad dog bites called for combining peppermint or spearmint with salt and applying it to the wound.

Given half a chance, mint will muscle its way throughout the garden, but you can keep it in check with barriers made from plastic pots. And don't be afraid to pull it out ruthlessly—it always grows back!

Variegated oregano is a low-growing beauty perfect for accenting other plants along the edge of the border.

OREGANOS
(*Origanum* spp.)

Tomatoes—and subsequently, tomato sauce—would only be half as popular without the biting flavor of oregano. This perennial herb is hardy in Zones 5 to 9 and grows to about 2 feet tall. Flavor varies with variety, so you might want to grow several different kinds to find the one (or two or three) that you like best.

Growing Guidelines

Grow oregano in full sun and well-drained, rich garden soil. Starting with plants is probably the best way to grow this herb because seedlings vary in flavor. (Starting with plants also allows you to

IN THE KITCHEN

OREGANO HAS A hot, peppery flavor and enhances lots of foods, including omelets, frittatas, and quiches. Oregano also adds dimension to

- eggplant
- mushrooms
- onions
- potatoes
- zucchini
- roasted bell peppers
- marinated vegetables
- beef
- pork
- poultry
- yeast breads

And, of course, oregano's flavor combines well with garlic, parsley, thyme, and olive oil.

taste before planting.) Space the plants 1 to 2 feet apart, and keep mulch away from the stems to promote air circulation and prevent disease problems. Divide the plants every 3 to 5 years.

Harvesting Hints

You can harvest fresh leaves all season, as long as the plants are growing vigorously. Stop harvesting 2 to 4 weeks before the first expected frost; dry the remainder of your harvest so that you can enjoy the flavor of this herb all winter long.

Trivia Tidbits

Many of oregano's early uses were medicinal, rather than culinary. For example, the Greeks made dressings from oregano leaves and placed them on sores and aching muscles, while some Roman scholars recommended oregano dressings for scorpion and spider bites. And after oregano was introduced to North America by European colonists, doctors used oil of oregano to help ease the pain of toothaches.

If you like pizza, then oregano is an indispensable herb for your garden. Cut and dry the leaves throughout the growing season to ensure a winter-long supply.

Curly parsley has frilly, dark green leaves that are mild in flavor. It's often used as a garnish.

PARSLEY

(Petroselinum crispum)

Parsley really has a lot more to offer than just being the token garnish on a plate of steak or fish. This herb is an excellent addition to most recipes, is rich in vitamins and minerals (A, C, calcium, and iron), and fights bad breath (the chlorophyll it contains is a natural breath sweetener). Parsley is a biennial grown as an annual; it will grow in Zones 5 through 9. You can choose from two parsley varieties: curly leaf and flat-leaved.

Growing Guidelines

Parsley grows best in rich, moist, well-drained soil in full sun to partial shade. Sow seeds outdoors when the soil temperature averages 50°F. You'll need some patience because parsley seed germinates extremely slowly, often requiring 6 weeks before the seedlings

 IN THE **KITCHEN**

PARSLEY HAS A gentle flavor and works especially well at blending the flavors around it. You can use both the curly and flat-leaved varieties in cooking, although flat-leaved parsley is more flavorful. You can add parsley to most foods (except sweets), including

- salsa
- grilled meats
- tabbouleh
- poultry
- ham

poke up through the soil. (You can speed germination by soaking the seeds in water overnight before planting.) Once the seedlings pop up, thin them to 8 to 10 inches apart.

Harvesting Hints

You can begin harvesting parsley as soon as the plants are growing vigorously. Snip individual outer stems from the plants; they'll continue to produce new growth all season long.

Parsley dries and freezes well. If you dry it, crush it by hand after it's completely dry and store it in an airtight container.

Trivia Tidbits

In ancient Greece, parsley was used in funeral ceremonies and to make wreaths for graves. Parsley was also placed in wreaths given to winning athletes because the Greeks believed that the god Hercules had chosen parsley for his garlands.

Flat-leaved or Italian parsley has the intense flavor prized by cooks. Swallowtail butterfly caterpillars find parsley pretty tasty, too.

ROSEMARY

(Rosmarinus officinalis)

Rosemary is an herb that's not just for the kitchen spice rack. You can use rosemary to make sachets for your drawers or a rinse for your hair. And rosemary oil adds a pleasant piney scent to soaps, creams, lotions, and toilet waters.

Rosemary grows in shrubby clumps of branching stems covered with wonderfully fragrant, needlelike, green leaves. This herb is a half-hardy perennial that's an evergreen in Zones 8

Rosemary is a versatile herb suitable for the garden, kitchen, and bath.

IN THE **KITCHEN**

ROSEMARY IS PUNGENT and somewhat piney. Its flavor harmonizes with poultry, fish, lamb, beef, and pork—particularly when these foods are roasted. Gentle soups benefit from rosemary's robust character, as do marinades, salad dressings, and cream sauces. Rosemary also enhances

- mushrooms
- peas
- spinach
- squash
- tomatoes
- lentils
- cheese
- eggs

You can use both the flowers and the leaves for garnishing and cooking. Crush or mince the spiky leaves before sprinkling over or rubbing into foods.

through 9. In Zones 6 and 7, you can grow the hardy variety 'Arp', or you can grow rosemary as a container plant that's overwintered indoors.

Plants can reach 5 to 6 feet tall where they're hardy outdoors; container plants reach 1 to 3 feet tall.

Growing Guidelines

This aromatic herb grows best in well-drained, sandy, or gravelly soil and full sun. Seedlings grow very slowly, so you'll want to buy plants and start with them for fastest results. Space plants 1 to 2 feet apart (if you plan to grow your rosemary as a perennial in the garden, space the plants a good 4 feet apart).

Harvesting Hints

You can continuously harvest rosemary as long as the plants are growing. Strip the needles from the stems, then chop them before using. Rosemary also dries and freezes well. Freeze whole sprigs, and when you need some leaves, slide your thumb and index finger down a sprig, taking off as many leaves as you need.

Though rosemary may grow to be shrub-size in warmer climes, it requires a bit of coddling in cooler zones. 'Arp' is a bit hardier (to Zone 6). Cold-zone gardeners will need to bring their rosemary indoors for the winter.

Trivia Tidbits

In ancient Greece, students wore rosemary garlands in their hair while studying for exams because they believed rosemary would help improve their memory. In the Middle Ages, men and women placed rosemary sprigs under their pillows to ward off demons and prevent bad dreams.

The dusty, blue-gray leaves of sage contrast nicely with dark foliage and brightly colored flowers in herb gardens and ornamental plantings.

SAGE
(Salvia officinalis)

If you can grow only one herb in your garden, you might want to make it sage. This shrubby perennial (about 2 feet tall) is an herb gardener's delight. The plants grow quickly without becoming invasive, and the flowers attract hummingbirds and beneficial insects. Sage is an intensely aromatic culinary herb that's hardy to Zone 5, but it will often survive in Zone 4 with winter protection.

Growing Guidelines

Sage thrives in average, well-drained soil in full sun. You can buy plants or grow your own from seed. If you grow your own, start the seeds indoors 6 to 8 weeks

IN THE KITCHEN

SAGE LEAVES HAVE a lemony, pungent taste and are the perfect complement to poultry, stuffings, and sausages, as well as

- artichokes
- potatoes
- asparagus
- squash
- eggplant
- tomatoes
- onions

You can add dried sage leaves to dishes, too. A bit of dried, crumpled sage, for example, perks up soft cheeses and lends an earthy tone to breads, especially flat breads like Italian focaccia.

before your last frost date. The seeds should germinate within 3 weeks at 60° to 70°F. Transplant the seedlings outdoors after all danger of frost has passed. Space the plants 18 to 24 inches apart in the garden.

Harvesting Hints

You can harvest sage leaves as long as the plants are actively growing. Sage leaves also dry and freeze well. To dry, snip the leaves from branches you've removed, discard the stems, and spread the leaves on cloth or paper in a dark, dry place. Store in an airtight container.

Trivia Tidbits

Native Americans used sage as a medicine, mixing it with bear grease for a salve they claimed would cure skin sores. They also used sage as a leafy, disposable toothbrush.

Common sage sends up whorls of lilac-blue flowers around the middle of summer. For the best flavor, harvest and dry the leaves before the flowers appear.

SAVORY, SUMMER
(Satureja hortensis)

Summer savory is an annual that's highly aromatic and has been used to enhance the flavor of food for over 2,000 years. It has tiny white or pale pink flowers and grows to 1½ feet high.

Growing Guidelines

This herb likes full sun and average soil and is easy to grow from seed. If you start summer savory from seed, keep in mind that it germinates quickly—so plan your planting accordingly. You can sow seeds no more than ½ inch deep in

Summer savory's uniquely flavored leaves are the perfect partner for many bean dishes.

IN THE KITCHEN

SUMMER SAVORY TASTES like peppery thyme and blends well with most flavors, helping to bring them together. It's popular in teas, herb butters, and flavored vinegars, as well as with

- asparagus
- garlic
- onions
- peas
- squash
- lentils
- soups
- eggs

This herb is also a nice accompaniment to fish. You can make a fish marinade by mincing fresh savory leaves and combining them with garlic, bay, and lemon juice. Or, add minced fresh savory to mayonnaise and serve it with poached fish.

flats and transplant later, or plant directly into the garden. Space plants about 10 inches apart and keep them well weeded and well watered. If the plants start to flop over, mound soil slightly around their bases.

Harvesting Hints

You can begin harvesting summer savory as soon as the plants get about 6 inches tall. If you keep snipping the tops of the branches, you'll be able to extend the harvest. When the plants insist on flowering, cut the whole plants and lay them on screening or paper in a warm, shady place. After they've dried (in a couple of days), strip the leaves from the stems and store the leaves in airtight jars. You can also collect the seeds as soon as they start to brown. Then place them in an airtight jar along with a desiccant (such as silica gel), and store the jar in a cool, dry place.

Trivia Tidbits

The Romans used savory extensively in their cooking, often flavoring vinegars with it. And the poet Virgil suggested growing savory near beehives because of the pleasant-tasting honey it produced.

A side-dressing of compost early in the season will help summer savory become established. Trim the plants regularly to keep the flavorful leaves in good supply.

With so many differently scented geraniums available, the most difficult challenge about growing them may be choosing which ones to grow! Rose-scented geranium is a popular choice.

SCENTED GERANIUMS
(*Pelargonium* spp.)

Apple, apricot, coconut, lemon, lime, peppermint, rose, strawberry—they sound like specialty lollipop flavors that you might find on a sweetshop counter. But these are just a few of the fragrances available in the amazing repertoire of scented geraniums.

These herbs aren't really geraniums at all, although their leaves look very similar to true geraniums. Scented geraniums are tender perennials that are hardy only in Zone 10. Some varieties can grow up to 3 feet high, while others are compact and work well in baskets. You can enjoy their fragrance in the garden, or dry the leaves and flowers to make sachets and potpourris.

Growing Guidelines

You'll have the best success with scented geraniums if you start with plants or cuttings from a friend.

IN THE KITCHEN

YOU CAN USE the leaves of rose geraniums to flavor sugar. Simply alternate layers of sugar and leaves in a mason jar, and place the jar where it will catch the sun for about 2 weeks. Then sift the leaves out and you'll have rose-flavored sugar. You can also use some varieties of scented geraniums to flavor

- tea
- jelly
- biscuits
- pound cake

If you choose cuttings, take them in spring or summer, using a sharp knife just below the node where a leaf grows from the stem. Place cuttings in clean sand, and allow enough space around them so that air can circulate freely. Keep them well watered (but not soggy), and in 2 to 3 weeks you should have little plants that you can transplant. Expose the plants to the outdoors only after the threat of frost is past.

Harvesting Hints

Pick leaves just as the flowers begin to appear—preferably on a sunny, dry, day—for maximum oil content. Dry leaves in the shade to preserve their fragrance.

Trivia Tidbits

Scented geraniums arrived in America during the colonial days and became popular rather quickly. Thomas Jefferson, in fact, brought several varieties to the White House with him.

The flowers of most scented geraniums (like the peppermint-scented type pictured below) aren't very showy, but their carefree habit and intensely fragrant leaves make them worthy additions to any herb garden.

Use tarragon to flavor wine vinegars or to add a spicy hint of licorice to fish and poultry dishes.

TARRAGON

(*Artemisia dracunculus* var. *sativa*)

Gardeners grow this aromatic, hardy perennial for its distinctively flavored leaves. Although tarragon isn't what most people would consider a visually stunning plant, it's definitely worth growing because it's such a versatile culinary herb. Tarragon reaches 2 feet tall and will grow in Zones 4 through 8.

Growing Guidelines

French tarragon needs full sun or partial shade and loose, rich, well-drained soil. Start by buying plants (French tarragon doesn't produce viable

IN THE KITCHEN

TARRAGON OFFERS A strong, unusual licorice flavor that stands out in cooked dishes. As a general rule, don't add this herb with a heavy hand, and don't cook it too long or else you'll bring out its bitter side. (For maximum flavor, add tarragon to long-cooking soups and stews during the last 15 minutes.) Just a few of the foods tarragon enhances are

- artichokes
- leeks
- peas
- potatoes
- rice
- beef and pork
- fish
- shellfish
- poultry

seed), or get divisions or cuttings from established herb gardens. Space the plants 1 to 2 feet apart. To get the best flavor from the foliage, remove the flower stems when they form. Divide plants every 3 to 5 years to keep them growing vigorously and to help them maintain their flavor.

Harvesting Hints

Harvest the foliage continuously as long as the plants are actively growing. If you want to store fresh tarragon, freeze it or preserve it in white vinegar (tarragon doesn't dry well).

You can also use this herb in flavored vinegars, herbed butters, cream sauces, and soups and with cheeses, eggs, sour cream, and yogurt.

Trivia Tidbits

Tarragon was thought to prevent fatigue, so pilgrims of the Middle Ages put sprigs of it in their shoes before beginning long trips on foot.

For the best tarragon flavor, be sure to purchase French tarragon plants (they can only be produced from divisions or cuttings). Pinch the leaves before you buy—if you smell a hint of anise, you know you've found the real thing.

Tiny thyme leaves pack big flavor that intensifies with drying. Dried leaves are up to three times more potent than fresh.

THYME
(*Thymus vulgaris*)

Thyme is an incredibly useful herb. You can use it in recipes or as a cough suppressant; it attracts beneficial insects, like bees; and it grows just as well on a windowsill as it does in your garden beds.

This perennial herb will grow in Zones 5 through 9 and reaches about 1 foot high. Although thyme comes in both upright and prostrate forms, you should choose upright varieties for using in cooking because low-growing types are often gritty with rain-splashed soil.

Growing Guidelines

A well-drained site with sandy soil in full sun to partial shade is ideal for thyme. Because thyme seed is rarely true to type, your best bet is to start with plants or divisions. Space new plants 12 inches apart.

IN THE KITCHEN

THE BITTERSWEET TASTE of thyme seems right for almost any dish, from vegetables and meats to soups and casseroles. Specifically, thyme works well with

- corn
- peas
- sweet peppers
- tomatoes
- rice
- cheese
- eggs

Its flavor also blends well with lemon, garlic, and basil.

Once established, thyme is easy to keep looking good and producing well. Prune it lightly as needed to maintain its attractive shape.

Harvesting Hints

For fresh use, pick individual leaves or small sprigs as needed. If you want to dry thyme, strip the leaves from the stems and place them on a thin screen to dry before storing. Thyme also freezes well—just make sure you use an airtight container.

Trivia Tidbits

From the fifteenth through the seventeenth centuries, thyme was used to combat the plagues that swept over Europe. And as recently as World War I, thyme's essential oil served as an antiseptic on the battlefields.

Trouble-free thyme is a staple of the kitchen herb garden. It requires little care as long as it's provided a sunny site with good drainage.

Your Seasonal Herb-Care Calendar

NOW THAT YOU know the basics of growing herbs organically, you'll need to know when to start seeds indoors, direct-sow seeds outdoors, mulch, and prune to give your herb plants conditions in which they can thrive. This calendar gives you, at a glance, what you'll need to do each month.

Also, keep in mind that because of climatic conditions, planting herbs in Florida isn't the same as planting them in Maine. Before you even start planning for herbs, you need to find out what hardiness zone you live in. (Check out the map on page 106.)

JANUARY

❄️ Although the weather outside may be snowy and cold, you can warm up with thoughts of your garden to come.

- Spend some time paging through gardening magazines and herb books to **collect ideas** for the upcoming season. Or check out the Web site: www.organicgardening.com.

- Read about all the different ways **you can use herbs** (in cooking, **as medicines**, and in cosmetics and crafts).

- **Inventory** your garden supplies to make sure you have the essentials, such as a trowel, a cultivator, and plant markers.

FEBRUARY

❄️ With spring around the corner, now is the time to start getting your garden plans together.

- **Finalize** which herbs you want to plant, and then decide **where to grow them**—in pots on your patio, on a kitchen windowsill, or in your vegetable garden or flowerbeds.

- Keep in mind that most perennial herbs like well-drained soil, so **cluster water lovers** (such as basil and parsley) together.

- **Buy seeds** for fast-growing annual herbs (like borage) to sow directly.

MARCH

✿ Now you can start to get your hands dirty!

- Remove protective **winter mulch** as you begin to see new growth on your perennial herbs.

- If you're planning on starting annual herbs from seed, now is the time to **plant those seeds** in flats.

- This month is also a good time to **select and prepare a site** for a new herb garden. An ideal place would be an area close to your house that gets at least 6 hours of full sunlight each day.

APRIL

✿ Plant new perennial herb plants. Trim woody herbs like **lavender** as they begin to show new growth. Start basil seedlings indoors for an earlier harvest.

MAY

✿ You'll have plenty to do this month in your herb garden.

- **Plant annual herbs** outdoors after your last frost date.

- **Direct sow seeds** for fast growers like dill and cilantro. To extend your

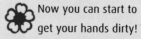

Winter   **Spring**   **Summer**   **Fall**

harvest, sow seeds successively every 2 weeks.

- You can also **plant tender perennial herbs**, such as scented geraniums and rosemary, outside, either in the ground or in pots.
- Dig up and **divide large clumps** of perennial herbs as necessary.
- **Mulch between plants** with compost, shredded bark, or another organic material.

JUNE

Continue to **sow** fast-growing annual herbs such as **borage** every 2 weeks. Harvest fresh herbs to add flavor to summertime dishes. **Pull out weeds** that crop up between your herbs.

JULY

During these lazy, hazy dog days of summer, you should:

- **Water** as necessary.
- **Hang sages and lavender** in a dry, dark place for later use in herbal wreaths.

- **Make** lots of **pesto** with your basil, cutting off flowerstalks as you harvest.
- Sit in the shade and **enjoy** a refreshing glass of mint **iced tea** (or a mint julep) made with mint you picked from your own plants.

AUGUST

Use your bounty of herbs to make flavored **vinegars and oils**. Sow seed for a later harvest of dill and cilantro. Continue to harvest, freezing or drying what you can't use now for use in winter.

SEPTEMBER

Dig up and **pot tender herbs** such as scented geraniums and rosemary. Let them adjust outdoors in their pots before bringing them in. Or **take cuttings** to root for next year's garden if you don't have space for whole plants.

OCTOBER

Fall signals the time to begin winding down. This month:

- **Clean up** the garden after Jack Frost has made his appearance.
- **Pull out spent annual herbs** and cut back any perennial herbs that need it.
- **Organize notes** you took from the gardening season and compile them in a binder, along with a map of where each herb grew.

NOVEMBER

Before the ground freezes, add a protective winter mulch of **shredded leaves** to perennial herbs. Enjoy the season's bounty by using your dried herbs for seasonings in recipes, creating potpourris, and **making wreaths**.

DECEMBER

Use **evergreen boughs** as additional winter protection by laying them over your perennial plants. **Give** friends and family **gifts of potpourris**, scented sachets, wreaths, and herbal vinegars that you made with herbs from your garden.

Herb Garden Glossary

Learning the lingo that goes with herb gardening will make your trips to the home and garden center that much easier. Here's a list of terms you're likely to come across in this book, as well as in the gardening aisles.

Air-dry. To preserve herbs for later use by hanging branches by their stems in a dark, airy place, or by drying them on racks through which air can circulate.

Annual. A plant that germinates, flowers, sets seed, and dies within 1 year.

Beneficial insects. Insects that have a positive effect on garden plants by preying on pest insects or by pollinating plants.

Biennial. A plant that takes 2 years to complete its life cycle.

Bouquet garni. Culinary herbs such as bay leaf, thyme, and parsley, tied in a small bunch and added to soups, stew, or sauces. The herbs are removed before serving.

Companion planting. Combinations of plants that work well together to repel pests, attract beneficial insects, or make efficient use of garden beds.

Compost. Decomposed or partially decomposed organic matter (such as kitchen scraps, leaves, grass clippings, and dead plants) that is dark in color and crumbly in texture. Used as an amendment, compost increases the water-holding capacity of the soil and is an excellent nutrient source for microorganisms, which later release nutrients to your plants.

Compost tea. A fertilizer made by soaking a cloth bag full of compost in a watering can or barrel for several days.

Culinary herbs. Herbs used in cooking.

Cutting. A 3- to 5-inch clipping of healthy green growth that is cut from the parent plant and placed in potting mix to root.

Direct seeding. Planting seeds outside directly into the garden.

Division. A way to propagate perennial herb plants by dividing established plants at the roots to form several new plants.

Dormancy. A resting phase for plants that enables them to survive conditions of cold, drought, or other stress, during which they may have no leaves or flowers.

Essential oils. Highly concentrated aromatic oils of plants that are used in cosmetic preparations.

Fish emulsion. An organic liquid fertilizer, made from fish solubles, that contains 4 to 5 percent nitrogen. It is used most often for foliar fertilization (where fertilizer is applied to and absorbed through the plant's leaves).

Full sun. Plants that thrive in full sun need a minimum of 6 hours of direct sun each day. Most herbs prefer a sunny location.

Hardening off. Gradually exposing tender seedlings to the outdoors in a protected area for a week prior to transplanting them into the garden.

Hardiness. Plants are able to tolerate varying levels of cold temperatures and still survive. Plant hardiness zones help gardeners determine which perennials will survive the winter in a specific area.

Herbaceous. A perennial plant that dies back to the ground at the end of each growing season.

Herbicide. A substance used to kill unwanted plants. Some types are selective (they kill only a certain type of plant); others are nonselective and will kill any plants they come into contact with.

Herb standard. A perennial or tender perennial herb plant that is trained to be a single stem with branches only at the top.

Insecticidal soap. A specially formulated solution of fatty acids that kills insect pests such as aphids, mites, and whiteflies.

Layering. Propagating a perennial plant by taking a stem, bending it to the ground, and burying it in the soil. New roots will form underground.

Mulch. Any material, organic or inorganic, used to cover the ground in order to preserve moisture and prevent the growth of weeds.

Organic. Materials that are derived directly from plants or animals. Organic gardening uses plant and animal byproducts to maintain soil and plant health and doesn't rely on synthetically made fertilizers, herbicides, or pesticides.

Perennial. Herbs are considered perennial if they last for 2 or more years.

Pesticide. A substance, synthetic or natural, that is used to kill insects, animals, fungi, or bacteria.

Potpourri. A scented mixture of dried herbs and flowers, spices, and essential oils.

Poultice. A soothing herbal paste made by mixing dried herbs with a small amount of hot water. Poultices are put directly on the skin and held in place with a warm cloth.

Rootbound. A condition that results from a plant outgrowing its container, so that the roots are densely crowded and often coiled around the inside of the pot.

Sachet. A fragrance bag made with a combination of dried herb leaves and (frequently) rose petals, crumbled or ground.

Seedling. A young plant grown from seed. Commonly, plants grown from seed are termed seedlings until they are first transplanted.

Self-sow. Herbs such as German chamomile, cilantro, and dill that will reseed themselves if left to go to seed.

Tender perennial. A perennial plant that is treated as an annual because it is being grown outside of its hardiness zone.

Umbels. Flowers, such as Queen Anne's lace, that all have stalks that are the same length and that emerge from the same place on the stem and form a flat-topped cluster.

Volunteers. Plants that grow spontaneously in the garden from a previous year's seeds.

Recommended Reading & Resources

Books & Periodicals

Brown, Deni. *Eyewitness Garden Handbooks: Garden Herbs*. New York: DK Publishing, Inc., 1998.

Creasy, Rosalind. *The Edible Herb Garden*. Boston, MA: Periplus Editions, 1999.

Duke, James, Ph.D. *The Green Pharmacy*. Emmaus, PA: Rodale, 1997.

Fisher, Kathleen. *Rodale's Essential Herbal Handbooks: Herbal Remedies*. Emmaus, PA: Rodale, 1999.

Gardner, Jo Ann. *Herbs in Bloom: A Guide to Growing Herbs as Ornamental Plants*. Portland, OR: Timber Press, 1998.

Gruenberg, Louise. *Rodale's Essential Herbal Handbooks: Herbal Home Hints*. Emmaus, PA: Rodale, 1999.

James, Tina. *Rodale's Essential Herbal Handbooks: Cooking with Herbs*. Emmaus. PA: Rodale, 1999.

Keville, Kathy, and Peter Korn. *Herbs for Health and Healing*. Emmaus, PA: Rodale, 1998.

Kowalchik, Claire, and William H. Hylton, editors. *Rodale's Illustrated Encyclopedia of Herbs*. Emmaus, PA: Rodale, 1987.

McClure, Susan. *The Herb Gardener*. Pownal, VT: Storey/Garden Way Publishing, 1996.

Michalak, Patricia. *Rodale's Successful Organic Gardening: Herbs*. Emmaus, PA: Rodale, 1995.

Organic Gardening magazine, Rodale, 33 East Minor Street, Emmaus, PA 18098.

Smith, Miranda. *Your Backyard Herb Garden*. Emmaus, PA: Rodale, 1997.

Sombke, Laurence. *Beautiful Easy Herbs*. Emmaus, PA: Rodale, 1997.

Tolley, Emelie, et al. *Herbs: Gardens, Decorations, and Recipes*. New York: Clarkson Potter, 1998.

Seeds, Plants & Supplies

Artistic Gardens/Le Jardin du Gourmet
P.O. Box 75
St. Johnsberry Center, VT 05863
Phone: (802) 748-1446
Fax: (802) 748-9592
Web site: www.kingcon.com/agljdg

Bountiful Gardens
18001 Shafer Ranch Rd.
Willits, CA 95490-9626
Phone/fax: (707) 459-6410
Web site: www.bountifulgardens.org

Capriland's Herb Farm
534 Silver St.
Coventry, CT 06238
Phone: (203) 742-7244

Companion Plants
7247 N. Coolville Ridge Rd.
Athens, OH 45701
Phone: (740) 592-4643
Fax: (740) 593-3092
Web site: www.companionplants.com

The Cook's Garden
P.O. Box 535
Londonderry, VT 05148
Phone: (800) 457-9703
Fax: (800) 457-9705
Web site: www.cooksgarden.com

The Gourmet Gardener
8650 College Blvd.
Overland Park, KS 66210
Phone: (913) 345-0490
Fax: (913) 451-2443

Johnny's Selected Seeds
1 Foss Hill Rd.
Albion, ME 04910-9731
Phone: (207) 437-4301
Fax: (800) 437-4290
Web site: www.johnnyseeds.com

Mountain Valley Growers
38325 Pepperweed Road
Squaw Valley, PA 93675
Phone: (559) 338-2775
Fax: (559) 338-0075
Web site: www.mountainvalleygrowers.com

Nichols Garden Nursery
1190 N. Pacific Hwy.
Albany, OR 97321-4580
Phone: (541) 928-9280
Fax: (541) 967-8406
Web site: www.nicholsgardennursery.com

Richters
357 Highway 47
Goodwood, Ontario, L0C 1A0, Canada
Phone: (905) 640-6677
Fax: (905) 640-6641
Web site: www.richters.com

Shady Acres Herb Farm
7815 Highway 212
Chaska, MN 55318
Phone: (612) 466-3391
Fax: (612) 466-4739
Web site: www.shadyacres.com

Shepherd's Garden Seeds
30 Irene St.
Torrington, CT 06790
Phone: (860) 482-3638
Fax: (860) 482-0532
Web site: www.shepherdseeds.com

Well-Sweep Herb Farm
205 Mt. Bethel Rd.
Port Murray, NJ 07865
Phone: (908) 852-5390
Fax: (908) 852-1649

Acknowledgments

Contributors to this book include Anna Carr, Catherine Cassidy, Ellen Cohen, Alice Decenzo, Diana Erney, Marjorie Hunt, Judith Benn Hurley, William H. Hylton, Claire Kowalchik, Cheryl Long, Susan Milius, Joanna Poncavage, Lawrence Sombke, Kirsten Whatley, and Kim Wilson.

Photo Credits

Rob Cardillo 2, 7 (top right), 7 (top left), 7 (middle), 15

David Cavagnaro 54, 60, 62, 66, 80, 86, 96

Rosalind Creasey 23, 43

Dency Kane vi, 21, 44

Mitch Mandel 6 (middle), 6 (bottom), 7 (bottom), 8 (bottom)

Alison Miksch 9, 10, 14, 18, 20, 24, 27, 31, 33, 34, 38, 39

Jerry Pavia 40, 85

John Peden 11

Susan A. Roth 12, 30

Martin Wall/Steven Foster Group 45, 52, 53, 69, 79, 83

Rachel Weill iv, 4, 26, 36, 42, 46, 48, 49, 50, 51, 55, 56, 57, 58, 61, 63, 64, 65, 67, 68, 70, 71, 72, 73, 74, 75, 76, 77, 78, 81, 82, 84, 87, 88, 89, 90, 91, 92, 93, 94, 95

Rick Wetherbee I, 17, 47,

Kurt Wilson 6 (top), 8 (top)

Location Credits

The Huntington Botanical Gardens, San Marino, California iv, 42, 46, 48, 49, 50, 51, 55, 56, 57, 58, 59, 61, 63, 64, 65, 67, 68, 70, 71, 72, 73, 74, 75, 76, 77, 78, 81, 82, 84, 87, 88, 89, 90, 91, 92, 93, 94, 95

Home of Margaret Hess, Los Angeles, California (herb garden designed by Sandy Kennedy) 4

Stylist Credits

Barbara Fritz 9, 10, 14, 18, 20, 24, 27, 31, 33, 34, 38, 39

Anneliese Gomez 4, 26

Index

L

Labels, 10
Lacewings, green, 3
Lady beetles, 3
Lavender *(Lavandula angustifolia)*
    profile, 68–69, *68, 69*
    sites for, 28
    uses for, 3, 17
Lemon balm *(Melissa officinalis)*
    growing, 26, 27
    profile, 70–71, *70, 71*
    sites for, 22, 31
    uses for, 16, 17, 20
Lemon thyme, 17
Lemon verbena *(Aloysia triphylla)*, 17,
    72–73, *72, 73*
Levisticum officinale, 14, 22, 74–75, *74, 75*
Lovage *(Levisticum officinale)*, 14, 22,
    74–75, *74, 75*

M

Marjoram *(Origanum majorana)*, 14, 26,
    76–77, *76, 77*
Matricaria recutita, 26, 52–53, *52*
Medicinal herbs, 19–20. *See also specific herbs*
Melissa officinalis
    growing, 26, 27
    profile, 70–71, *70, 71*
    sites for, 22, 31
    uses for, 16, 17, 20
Mentha spp.
    as companion plant, 22, 23
    profile, 78–79, *78, 79*
    sites for, 22, 31
    uses for, 3, 17
Microwave drying, 39
Mint *(Mentha* spp.)
    as companion plant, 22, 23
    profile, 78–79, *78, 79*
    sites for, 22, 31
    uses for, 3, 17
Mint water, 78
Mulch, 11, 28, 29
Mustard, 26

N

Nepeta cataria
    as companion plant, 22
    growing, 26
    profile, 50–51, *50, 51*
    sites for, 22
    uses for, 16, 17
Nursery pots, to control invasives, 8–9, *8,* 28

O

Ocimum basilicum
    as companion plant, 23, *23*
    freezing, 37
    growing, 26
    profile, 46–47, *46, 47*
    uses for, 2, *2,* 13, *14,* 19
Oregano *(Origanum* spp.)
    profile, 80–81, *80, 81*
    sites for, 28
    uses for, 14
Origanum majorana, 14, 26, 76–77, *76, 77*
Origanum spp.
    profile, 80–81, *80, 81*
    sites for, 28
    uses for, 14
Oven drying, 38, *38*

P

Parsley *(Petroselinum crispum)*
    growing, 26
    harvesting, 35
    profile, 82–83, *82, 83*
    sites for, 31
    storing, *36*
    uses for, 3, 14, 20
Pelargonium spp.
    as companion plant, 22
    fragrance, releasing, *16*
    profile, 90–91, *90, 91*
    traditional meaning, 19
    uses for, 17
Perennials. *See also specific herbs*
    harvesting, 35–36
    planting, 26–28
    preparing for winter, 29–31
Pest control, herbs for, 22
Pesticides, 2

USDA Plant Hardiness Zone Map

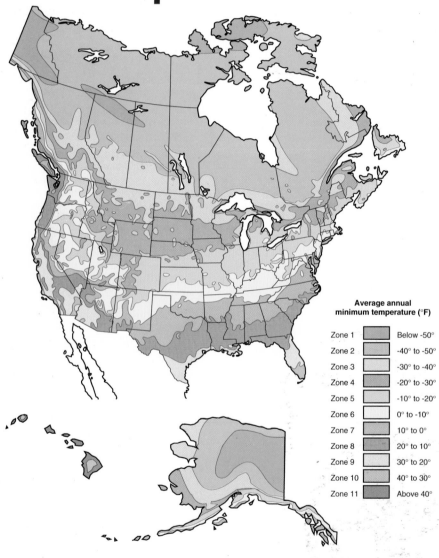

Average annual minimum temperature (°F)

Zone 1		Below -50°
Zone 2		-40° to -50°
Zone 3		-30° to -40°
Zone 4		-20° to -30°
Zone 5		-10° to -20°
Zone 6		0° to -10°
Zone 7		10° to 0°
Zone 8		20° to 10°
Zone 9		30° to 20°
Zone 10		40° to 30°
Zone 11		Above 40°

This map was revised in 1990 and is recognized as the best indicator of minimum temperatures available. Look at the map to find your area, then match its color to the key. When you've found your color, the key will tell you what hardiness zone you live in. Remember that the map is a general guide; your particular conditions may vary.